HEALING WHILE BLACK

Ancient Wisdom, Modern Psychology, and
the Science of Healing

Natasha Ickes

Table of Contents

Dedication

I dedicate this book to my children, Kamaya and Esteban Jr.

Because of you, I am.

You are the reason I reach higher, love deeper, and refuse to shrink. May you always know the brilliance you carry and the ancestors who walk with you.

To every Black child — grown or growing — searching for themselves in a world that doesn't always see them: may these pages remind you of your strength, your story, and the unshakable brilliance written into your bones.

And for every Black soul seeking healing, wholeness, and home within themselves — may you remember your power, your lineage, and the light that will never be dimmed.

Introduction

This book exists because our true story deserves to be told. It is my attempt to honor that truth by naming why healing as a Black person can feel so exhausting — even when you're doing "all the right things."

Healing While Black blends ancient wisdom, modern psychology, and cutting-edge science. Together, they reveal how stress, trauma, and oppression shape the mind, body, and spirit.

Take this as an invitation to reclaim your peace, health, and power. By the end of this journey, you'll walk away with practical tools that support healing in your real, everyday life.

This is not a book you simply read- it is a book you experience.

Inside, you'll learn:

- how historical trauma shapes mental and physical health
- why stress and trauma live in the body — and how to release them
- how belief, breath, movement, and community support healing
- how to regulate your nervous system and reconnect with inner wisdom
- how to build a life rooted in joy, purpose, and freedom

Throughout each section, you'll find short, practical exercises designed to help you integrate the work — not just understand it. Healing isn't a concept; it's a practice and a daily act of choosing yourself.

By the end of this book, you'll walk away with:

- a clear understanding of the psychological impact of being Black in America
- tools to restore your mind, strengthen your body, and reconnect with your spirit
- and a framework for building a future rooted not in survival — but in freedom

To heal as a Black person in America is an act of resistance. This journey is personal and it belongs to you.

As Maya Angelou once said, *"You may not control all the events that happen to you, but you can decide not to be reduced by them."*

Let's begin.

"They tried to bury us. They didn't know we were seeds."

— *Mexican Proverb*

PART I

THE
WOUNDS
WE CARRY

Brown Skin

Skin like butter toffee, smooth as silk, kissed by the sun.
Milk chocolate richness, deep as the earth. Brown skin.

Often judged. Mislabeled. Outcast.
Lazy. Unworthy. Disgusting.
The whispers, the weight, the burden—brown skin.

Fetishized.
Run. Jump. Rap. Sing. Perform.
But do it quietly—no thoughts, no voice.
Just take it. Brown skin.

They forget—
This skin carries warriors in its marrow.
Strength in its bones.
Power in its DNA.
A survivor's bloodline. Brown skin.

We have fought, innovated, built, and rebuilt.
We have learned, taught, wept, and created.
We are the blueprint. Brown skin.

Mothers of civilization, daughters of the stars.
The seed of all that was, the essence of all that is.
Unparalleled beauty, unwavering strength.
Empathy, intuition, wisdom—simply unmatched.
Brown skin.

I believe in reincarnation.
That we choose before we come.
That we walk into this world knowing—
This path is not easy.

This soul is here to shake the ground.
To take on what others would not survive.
To build where many would crumble.
To preserve, no matter what.
Brown skin.

A legacy of warriors.
A people who refuse to break.
We do not settle.
We cannot be silenced.

And no matter what—still, we rise.
Brown skin.

Speckled with gold.
Sun-warmed, earth-rooted, fire-forged.
Brown skin.

-Natasha Ickes

To heal, we first have to tell the truth.

That means naming the wounds we carry, facing the history that shaped them, and refusing the watered-down stories America has handed us. For generations, our history has been whitewashed, diminished, or erased. And when you erase a people's history, you attempt to erase their dignity, their memory, and the truth of who they have always been. But we have always been more than what was done to us.

Part One is about reclaiming what was stolen — not just our bodies, but our narrative.

It's about understanding the ways trauma has been passed down through our families, our health, our wealth, and even our sense of self. And it's about honoring the power, creativity, and resilience that have carried us through every generation.

Because no matter the country or continent, our story has never been one of defeat.

It has always been one of survival, brilliance, and becoming.

We cannot — and will not — be erased.

"Rain does not fall on one roof alone.
And no matter how long the winter,
spring is sure to follow"

— *African Proverb*

Chapter 1

Roots

Half-Truths and Erasure

When my daughter was in the 3rd grade, she came home with a worksheet: "10 Facts About MLK Jr." Fill-in-the-blank style: He was born on __, he was married to __, he had __ kids. Cute — but missing the whole truth. I grabbed a sharpie and made her write one more fact at the very top: *The U.S. government was found responsible for his assassination.* Then I told her to get up in front of the class the next day and say it out loud.

She looked confused and asked "Why?". My answer was simple: "To whom much is given, much is required. When you have knowledge, it's your duty to share it."

In 1999, a Memphis jury heard a wrongful death case brought by the King family against Loyd Jowers, who claimed he had been part of a conspiracy that involved government agencies. After four weeks of testimony from more than 70 witnesses, the jury unanimously concluded that Jowers and unnamed "co-conspirators including governmental agencies" were liable for Dr. King's assasination. The King family was awarded a symbolic $100 in damages [1]. For comparison, families of victims of the September 11 attacks received compensation that often totaled millions of dollars through federal victim compensation funds. Of course they don't teach that during Black History Month.

When my son came home talking about Rosa Parks several years later, I was just as frustrated with the way her story had been watered down. Too often she's described as a tired woman who couldn't bear to give up her seat on a bus. The truth? She was a trained activist and freedom fighter making a deliberate, strategic choice that would help shift the course of history. Rosa Parks herself said, *"I was not tired physically … the only tired I was, was tired of giving in"* [2].

See, America gives us half-truths, and if we're not careful, those become the only version people know. Today we're watching another wave of erasure —

history books being rewritten, entire lessons removed. A government hell bent on taking us backwards, openly spewing racist rhetoric and employing catastrophic policies. It is up to us to stay informed and to pass knowledge down to future generations. As Zora Neale Hurston said, "If you are silent about your pain, they'll kill you and say you enjoyed it."

To understand the depth of those wounds, we can't start with slavery alone. We must go back further — before the chains, before the ships, before the false narratives. Because our story doesn't begin in bondage. It begins in Africa, with civilizations that birthed knowledge, philosophy, medicine, and culture long before America ever knew our names.

Before the Chains

"Africa was the cradle of humanity and one of the first regions where organized societies, science, philosophy, and governance emerged." - UNESCO

Most Africans who were brought to America on the transatlantic slave route came from West Africa, or at least left from ports along the West African coast —

many through Ghana's infamous "Door of No Return" at Cape Coast and Elmina Castles. However, our story begins way before then. We come from an ancestry of philosophers, scholars, astronomers, scientists, healers, mothers, fathers, kings, and queens. Before we talk about what was done to us, we have to remember who we were — whole, brilliant, and free.

Long before Europe's so-called Enlightenment, the Mali Empire (14th–16th century) in West Africa produced kings so wealthy that Mansa Musa is still considered the richest man in history. On his pilgrimage to Mecca in 1324, he distributed so much gold that it disrupted economies across Africa and the Middle East [3].

Timbuktu, within the Mali Empire, was home to the legendary University of Sankoré, a center of learning that housed hundreds of thousands of manuscripts on medicine, astronomy, mathematics, law, and philosophy [4]. Many of these texts still survive today, standing as proof that Africa was not a "dark continent" before colonization, but a place where scholarship, science, and spiritual inquiry flourished.

And here's the part that always gets me: when you walk into most museums, the "African section" usually looks primitive (drums, masks, spears) while the European sections showcase paintings, sculptures, books, and inventions. While I am not devaluing what we see, it is not the full story and I believe this misrepresentation is purposeful. As Chancellor Williams the historian said, "Africa was civilized long before Europe and Asia, and Africa was teaching the world when Europe was learning to read."

African societies had systems of governance, trade routes, art, storytelling traditions, and spiritual practices that were complex and deeply rooted in community [5]. They were just as advanced, and often surpassed, anything in Europe. But you rarely see *that* displayed behind the glass. In fact, as recently as 2012, when extremists threatened to destroy Timbuktu's heritage, a Malian librarian named Abdel Kader Haidara risked his life to secretly move nearly 350,000 of these manuscripts to safety [6]. He packed centuries of knowledge—histories, poetry, astronomy, science—into metal footlockers and smuggled them hundreds of miles south to Bamako, one small cart at a time, in a covert mission that felt more like a spy thriller than a heritage operation. His bravery reminds us that our history has always been worth protecting.

And the more I learned about this legacy, the more something inside me ached to see it for myself — not through textbooks or museum glass, but with my own eyes and feet on the soil of my ancestors.

That longing to "go home" stayed with me for years. Finally, in 2023, I traveled to Africa for the first time. I took my son along on a trip to deliver my fourth TEDx talk, this one in Zimbabwe. It was a beautiful and life-changing experience. We went on safaris, explored crowded cities, ate in 5 star restaurants and met amazing people. We visited South Africa where monkeys climbed on our heads, and visited Tanzania where we stood at the largest slave port on the East African coast.

I wanted my son to see both the richness of who we are, and the weight of what was done to us. As we bent forward to squeeze into small stone cells that were once crammed with enslaved people my heart began to pound. Bars covered the tiny windows, and the air felt thick and stifling. I gripped my son's hand tighter as I imagined small children clinging to their mothers, terrified and uncertain of what was to come.

The guide pointed towards a separate cell down the hall which once held dozens of men at a time. I could almost taste the fear and feel the rage that lingered in the air from hundreds of years of men fighting against shackles- wrists and ankles bloody- desperate to break free to protect their families.

Each cell had two narrow stone ledges along the walls where bodies were forced to lie, shoulder to shoulder. The narrow strip of space in the center — what should have been a walkway — was used as a place to urinate and defecate. The smell must have been unbearable. I could almost hear the cries, feel the fear, and sense the despair lingering in the walls, as if the souls of those who suffered there still hadn't found rest.

When we finally stepped back into the sunlight, I held my son's hand a little tighter. We were walking out free— and they did not.

Joy and sorrow often live side by side and this trip was no different. It was agonizing, but also proof that even systems built to erase us could not win. As we left, I couldn't stop thinking about how their bloodline lived on in us. To make sense of that survival, I had to understand what they endured, and how the system that stole them grew into one of the most brutal in history.

See, unlike the West African ports that routed enslaved Africans across the Atlantic, this site was part of the Indian Ocean slave trade that sent people primarily to the Middle East. In the museums and archives, I learned truths that textbooks in America rarely teach: slavery in Africa, while still brutal, often looked very different from the chattel slavery practiced in the Americas. Enslaved people in parts of Africa could sometimes marry, own property, or even buy their freedom.

Everything changed with the arrival of Europeans. They exploited local conflicts, armed rival tribes, and forced leaders into trading captives. I doubt many could have imagined the horrors of what they were entering — a permanent, generational, dehumanizing system that would become the foundation of the Americas. But even in the face of chains and terror, our people refused to be broken. Resistance rose up again and again — sometimes quiet, sometimes explosive, but always there.

Rebellions of Resistance

The transatlantic slave trade operated on a scale and brutality the world had never seen, reducing human lives to cargo and profit. And still, they found ways to resist, endure, and remain human in a system designed to erase them.

Enslaved Africans braided escape maps into their hair and hid seeds in their cornrows, using creativity and intelligence as tools of survival. They sang spirituals that doubled as coded directions for freedom. Freedom fighters like Harriet Tubman returned again and again to liberate her people, while the Haitian Revolution shook the world as the first successful slave revolt that established a free Black republic.

Resistance didn't stop there — it rose up on plantations across the South, led by ordinary people who dared to defy an impossible system.

Nat Turner's rebellion of 1831 was a story that captivated me. Turner was a preacher, carried from plantation to plantation to deliver sermons that were meant to make slaves docile and obedient. By cherry picking and twisting certain bible verses, slaveholders tried to brainwash slaves and use religion as a means of control. But as Turner learned to read the Bible for himself, he began to see how its words had been weaponized. Through that he came to believe he was divinely appointed to rise up against slavery [7].

In August of 1831, he led one of the most significant slave rebellions in American history. Turner and a small group of followers moved from plantation to plantation in Southampton County, Virginia, killing about 55 slave holders and their families in an attempt to dismantle the system that had enslaved them. Though the rebellion was brutally suppressed within days, and Turner himself was captured and executed, the impact was seismic. The revolt sent shockwaves through the South, spreading fear among slaveholders and sparking even harsher laws designed to control enslaved and free Black people.

What's designed to destroy us often becomes the source of our strength. Over and over, our people have turned pain into power and pressure into purpose. Turner's rebellion reminds us that resistance has never been passive — it's always been deliberate, often dangerous, and always costly. Yet without people like him daring to act, we wouldn't have the blueprint of defiance that fuels our struggle today.

And Turner was not alone. Long before and long after his rebellion, others rose with the same unshakable fire.

The Stono Rebellion of 1739, in South Carolina, began with just 20 enslaved Africans. They raided a store for weapons and marched south toward Spanish Florida, where freedom had been promised to fugitives. Along the way, their numbers grew to nearly 100. This was not simply escape — though there is no shame in choosing to run. These men and women burned plantations, killed nearly 30 colonists, and marched with a purpose. The rebellion was eventually crushed, but it was one of many examples of our people organizing, strategizing, and refusing to accept the conditions forced upon them [8].

Even the German Coast Uprising of 1811 in Louisiana, the largest slave revolt in U.S. history — is one you've probably never heard about. Between 200 and 500 enslaved Africans marched along the Mississippi River toward New Orleans with makeshift weapons, flags, and drums, chanting for freedom.

They were met with violent suppression; many were killed, and their severed heads were displayed on pikes along the river as a warning. Still, the message couldn't be silenced.

Over and over again, enslaved Africans rose up, proving that resistance wasn't an isolated act of bravery but a recurring rhythm of defiance running through our history.

Legacies of Survival

After slavery was outlawed, some ships still smuggled enslaved Africans into the United States. In 1860 — more than 50 years after the transatlantic slave trade was officially banned — a ship called the *Clotilda* docked illegally in Mobile, Alabama, carrying 160 captives. Among them was Oluale Kossola, later known as Cudjo Lewis, believed to be the last survivor of the slave trade. After emancipation, Cudjo and other freed Africans pooled their resources, purchased land, and built their own community. Outsiders called it Africatown, and it still exists today as a living testament to survival, culture, and legacy. What made Africatown remarkable wasn't just that it existed, but that its founders preserved their African traditions — keeping their language, honoring their customs, and living in extended family units, passing down identity even in a foreign land.

While Africatown showed what it meant to keep traditions alive, other freedom fighters found resistance in different forms. Survival can be a village built from scratch — or one woman outsmarting an entire system.

Just look at Mary Ellen Pleasant — a woman who demonstrated resistance through strategy, intelligence, and financial power. Born around 1814, Pleasant moved to San Francisco during the Gold Rush and became one of the wealthiest Black women of her time. She built a fortune through savvy investments in businesses, real estate, and boarding houses, often using her wealth to quietly fund abolitionist causes. Historians even credit her with financing John Brown's raid on Harpers Ferry. Quite fittingly, she once declared, *"I'd rather be a corpse than a coward"*. She was fearless, unapologetic, and determined to wield her influence for the freedom of her people. But like so many powerful Black women, her legacy was twisted by racism and sexism. Instead of being remembered as a mogul and abolitionist, she was smeared with the nickname "Mammy Pleasant" in an attempt to strip her of dignity and reduce her accomplishments. Yet the truth endures: she was a strategist, a freedom fighter, and a woman far ahead of her time.

Stories like these remind us that even when the system tried to erase us, we carved out space for ourselves — building, preserving, resisting, and thriving in ways both big and small. But as slavery gave way to "freedom," another system rose in its place: Jim Crow. Slavery may have ended on paper, but oppression simply put on a new mask.

Jim Crow: The System After the Chains

We have all heard of Jim Crow and the laws that claimed "separate but equal." We also know this was a blatant lie — Black systems were deliberately underfunded, subpar, and unequal. The thing many people don't realize is how those laws and practices directly shape our lives today. And why, when people say we are living in the past, they simply have no idea how this country was built and continues to run.

Trauma wasn't just personal; it was written into the law of the land. Schools for Black children often received only a fraction of the funding of white schools — in some Southern states, less than one-third per student [9]. Even now, school funding relies heavily on property taxes. Because Black families were historically excluded from owning property in high-value neighborhoods through practices like redlining, predominantly Black schools remain underfunded[10]. Black children often get teachers who are overworked, underpaid and don't have access to the same resources that wealthier schools take for granted. In many ways, their education has always been set up as a pipeline — not toward opportunity, but toward prison or the most undesirable jobs in our communities

And it didn't stop at the classroom. Segregation extended into every corner of life. Even something as simple as a swimming pool was deliberately kept out of reach. This was not a social inconvenience. Swimming is a life-saving skill that we rarely had access to. Even now, Black children ages 10-14 drown in swimming pools at rates nearly eight times higher than White children [11].

I don't just know that from statistics — I know it from experience. I've saved two people from drowning. The second time I was an adult, but the first time, I was only a child.

Once, when my cousins and I were on vacation with my grandma, we all begged to get in the water. She was hesitant because she couldn't swim and of course was scared that something might happen to us. However, we eventually wore her down and she let us go in. After a while I was tired and got out of the water to sit with my grandma. All of a sudden we heard splashing, then looked over and noticed my younger cousin Kia. She was stuck in a bright plastic floaty tube, her little arms flailing as she tried to push herself free. Each time she kicked, the tube tilted and her head slipped beneath the water. She'd resurface with wide, panicked eyes, coughing and flailing, only to go under again. My grandma froze, terrified that if she jumped in, they might both drown. I dove in, swam under Kia, and pushed her up, breaking her free of the float.

As a child, I didn't grasp how close we came to tragedy — how all of our lives could have changed in an instant. In fact, I forgot it even happened. Decades later, after saving my stepdaughter from drowning, I was telling *that* story at Thanksgiving. Kia looked at me and said, "It's like when you saved me." I had to ask her to retell it, because the memory had completely slipped my mind.

But that's the thing about memory and survival: what feels small in the moment can reveal a much larger truth when you step back.

And when you zoom out, you start to see it's not just about one memory, one family, or one pool — it's about America itself. We live in a society that tells us to "get over it", stop living in the past, everything is equal now, slavery was so long ago, stop making everything about race.

But that's willful ignorance. The truth is, today is directly shaped by what our ancestors endured. We have an entire demographic who is still benefiting off decades of injustice, while we are still fighting against unfair systems of oppression. And what often threatens people most is this: we didn't just slip through the cracks they left for us. We broke down doors. We stepped onto stages. We shattered records. We raised the bar so high, the same system that tried to bury us now has to crane its neck just to watch us soar.

As a child, I remember sitting cross-legged in front of the TV, eyes glued to the screen, watching Surya Bonaly — the Black French ice skater who was the first to ever do a back flip on the ice. She defied every box they tried to put her in. She didn't just skate; she attacked the ice with a kind of fearlessness that made you sit up straighter. Her routines were powerful, athletic, and unapologetically different in a sport that often rewarded delicate, balletic "sameness." And then, to top it off, she was the first ever to do a back-flip on the ice. Imagine a crowded Olympic arena, lights bright, ice glistening, and an entire audience holding their breath as she launched herself into the air — not just flipping, but landing on one blade. Per-fect. Flawless. The crowd erupted, but the judges didn't know what to do with her brilliance. Instead of celebrating it, they banned the move entirely. Years later, when a white male skater attempted a version of the same trick, it was treated like a novelty- bold and definitely not punished.

For me, watching as a young Black girl, it was per-sonal. I was a competitive ice skater for several years, and the rink became a second home. You spend hours there training, and of course you become friends with the other kids. I'll never forget one local competition: I poured my heart out on the ice, giving it everything I had. Not long after, another skater — a young blonde, and someone who was really good — took her turn. When she finished, she came and stood next to me and the other competitors. All the girls we knew from the rink ran to her, hugging her, cheering her on, and gushing.

"You were so good!"

"Oh my God you just won!"

"You're amazziiinnnggggg!"

Not one of them looked my way, offered a hug, or even said good job. I stood right next to her but felt awkward and invisible. I smiled anyway, hugged her, and told her she had it as my heart sank.

Finally they started to announce the results. Fifth, fourth and third places were called. We glanced at each other nervously- we were the final two.

After a long pause "Annnnnndddd in second place.....". I could barely contain my excitement as she walked to the podium.

I did it, I won.

I still have the photo of me smiling ear to ear, the only black girl on the podium, back straight, head held high with the gold medal around my neck.

Looking back, I see it wasn't just about skating. It was about something bigger: who gets celebrated, who gets overlooked, and how race shapes those moments in ways we can't always name as kids. With Surya, I saw it play out on the world stage — how Black brilliance can awe the world and threaten the system so much that the only response is to change the rules to contain it.

Her backflip was in 1998, and nearly two decades later the same dynamic was still on display. Recently, a video went viral when the winner of the 2025 Miss International Queen pageant (a Black woman) was ignored after she won. Normally, the winner is the one who gets swarmed with hugs and congratulations. This time, almost every contestant rushed to the runner-up, a white woman, while the winner stood alone. Only one person walked over to acknowledge her.

I immediately thought back to my own experience as a child. I knew personally how that feels. For me it was smaller, but still an example of the ways our worth can be dismissed even when we win.

And here's the point: Jim Crow wasn't just laws written in books. It was a mentality, a whole system designed to suffocate us in every way — in the classroom, in the pool, on the farm, at the hospital, even on the ice. But it wasn't only about keeping us out of spaces; it was about cutting off the very resources needed to survive.

Economic Warfare and Medical Apartheid

To understand the true weight of Jim Crow, you can't just hear individual stories of injustice, or even picture the signs that said "colored" or "white." You have to follow the trail — the money, the medicine and the policies that touched every part of Black life. Because when you control people's resources and their health, you control their future. And when you create the systems, you decide who can build wealth and who will be permanently shut out of it.

By the early 20th century, Black Americans had built thriving farming communities, owning millions of acres of land and sustaining entire families and towns through agriculture. That level of independence was seen as a threat. As a result, Black farmers were not only systematically denied loans and subsidies from the USDA, they were also actively dispossessed of their land through fraud, coercion, and outright violence. White farmers and local officials often seized Black-owned land, and those who resisted faced intimidation, arson, and in many cases, lynching. By the 1990s, Black farmers had lost 90% of their land, much of it due to state-sanctioned discrimination and racial terror [12]. Today, the racial wealth gap and the lack of Black generational land ownership trace directly back to these policies.

And if choking off our wealth wasn't enough, the system also came for our bodies. Medical apartheid became another way of deciding who lived and who died. Black patients were excluded from white hospitals or relegated to segregated wards with little access to adequate care. In many towns, if a Black person was in a car accident, the nearest hospital would refuse them — sometimes resulting in death before they could reach a "colored ward" miles away. Then there's the infamous Tuskegee Syphilis Study (1932–1972), where hundreds of Black men were deliberately denied treatment so the government could "observe" how the disease progressed. Even after penicillin became the standard cure, they were left to suffer, sicken, and die while researchers took notes [13]. I can't fathom the cruelty of watching people suffer and die, while you hold the cure.

In other cases, Black bodies weren't neglected — they were used.

Henrietta Lacks — a Black woman and mother of five — went into Johns Hopkins Hospital in 1951 for treatment. Without her knowledge or consent, doctors took her cells. Unlike any others before them, Henrietta's cells continued to reproduce endlessly. They became the foundation of modern medicine [14] used in developing the polio vaccine, cancer treatments, IVF, and even COVID-19 research. Meanwhile, her family struggled for decades in poverty, unable to afford the very health care her cells were helping to revolutionize. Because of course, leave it to a Black woman to literally have magic cells that change the world, and still not get the recognition (or the hospital bill covered).

These are not just stories of the past. They are reminders that medical distrust in Black communities is not paranoia, it's lived experience. When your grandmother whispers, "Don't let them test things on you," or when families hesitate to participate in research trials, it isn't superstition. It's history and survival talking.

And I've experienced it firsthand. I was a young mom when I had my first child at 20. After 26 hours of contractions, I finally broke down and asked for an epidural. A white doctor walked in and said, "Hi, I'm the supervising physician, and Emily, the resident, will be giving you your epidural today." I looked up, exhausted, and between contractions replied, "Emily will be watching you give the epidural today."

Now, don't get me wrong — I know everyone has to learn somewhere. But I also know they pick and choose who they practice on. Seeing me, a young Black woman in Oakland, they thought they could tell me (not even ask) that I'd be today's test subject. They had the wrong one. Needless to say, Emily watched.

Even later, after being awake for nearly 37 hours straight, I finally dozed off. My daughter started crying and I didn't budge. A nurse came in, stood over me, and barked, "You need to wake up and feed her!" Before I could respond she spat out "You are a mother now". I will never forget the look of disgust on her face in a moment where all I needed was compassion and care. A kind word, gentle touch and warm demeanor would have created a totally different experience.

That's the thing about survival — sometimes it isn't just about getting through childbirth, or a hospital stay, or a single moment. It's about navigating systems that are built to dismiss us, belittle us, or break us. And that's where our instincts come in.

"When the roots are deep,
there is no reason to fear the wind."

— *African Proverb*

Chapter 2

Survival Instincts

Survival didn't just come from fighting laws or policies. It came from something deeper, something inside us- a wisdom we carry in our bones. I always say our intuition is a gift from God and the Universe — a way of tapping into a shared collective wisdom that we all hold inside. And for many Black folks, this is so much deeper than a "gut feeling." It is a survival mechanism passed down, the reason we are still here. I know, because it has saved my life more than once.

One night, less than a year after opening my salon, I went out with friends to a club in San Francisco. We were young, with dresses so short we spent half the night tugging them down. The kind where my grandma always said, *"Baby, if you drop something, just leave it there."* We had some drinks and were laughing, just enjoying ourselves.

Then all of a sudden the energy shifted.

Arguing broke out, voices got louder, and suddenly two groups of men — 15 or 20 on each side — squared off in the middle of the dance floor. The crowd parted like the Red Sea, everyone backing up, waiting for the spark. And let me tell you, in the Bay, sparks turn to fire quickly.

Instead of calming it down, the DJ made it worse. He played a song that sent the tension through the roof. 30 seconds into the song they started fighting. Fists flew, bottles shattered and people screamed. Then came the words that can change everything in an instant: *"Gun! He has a gun!"*

Chaos. Panic. People ran for the doors, desperate to escape while the two groups of men were in a full-on standoff. I watched one man run into the kitchen and come back clutching a butcher knife while another waved a gun.

Now, the logical move was to run. But, clear as day, I heard it: *Don't go outside those doors.*

I looked up and saw one of my friends stumbling toward the exit, dazed. I sprinted over, grabbed her arm, and yanked her back inside. Then I spotted a tiny alcove — barely enough space for us to crouch in but we managed to fit. Seconds later, the security guard slammed the doors shut, locking us inside.

I dropped down, my back against the wall, praying. My whole body was shaking and all I could think was: *My child needs me. PLEASE God! Let me get home to her!*

Everyone around us was desperate to live. People hid in bathrooms, behind the bar and in every corner they could find.

My best friend was locked outside of the club, crouching to the ground, terrified. A woman next to her screamed, "Are we going to die?", but no one had an answer.

Minutes dragged like hours. Then — *bam bam bam* — pounding on the doors. *"Open up! It's SFPD!"*

As we left the club I was grateful to be alive. I just wanted to go home. But when I got closer to my car I suddenly stopped. Police tape stretched across the street. A man had been shot just feet from where I was parked. My car was part of the crime scene.

If I had followed the crowd, I would've walked straight into the line of fire. If I would've done the "logical" thing and run to my car to get out of there, I may not be writing these words today.

That night branded the lesson onto me: intuition isn't just a feeling — it's protection.

It's helpful for everyone, but for Black folks that "sixth sense" isn't optional. It's the voice that tells you when to leave, when to stay, who to trust and who to avoid. It's wisdom written into our bones, born from centuries of survival. Neuroscientists describe this as the amygdala response: the brain's alarm system activating before the rational mind can catch up. From lynchings to Jim Crow to police violence, we learned to live in hypervigilance. And we pass it down — in "the talk" we give our children, in the way our bodies stiffen at flashing red and blue lights.

But here's the beauty in it: the same instincts born from trauma are also proof of resilience. Intuition is a spiritual inheritance. It's our connection to God, to the

Source, to the eternal wisdom that whispers before we even know why.

Science backs this up.

When our ancestors lived under constant threat, their nervous systems adapted. Cortisol and adrenaline fired so often that hypervigilance became almost second nature. Over time, this wasn't just "stress". It reshaped the body, tuning us to pick up on the smallest shifts in energy or behavior. Science now refers to this process as epigenetics, showing that trauma can literally change how genes are expressed, shaping how descendants respond to stress [15]. For Black communities, the fear and vigilance born from slavery, segregation, and ongoing racialized violence can show up generations later as anxiety, hypertension and chronic stress. It can also show up as a gut instinct that saves lives.

Because of this, I teach my children to use their intuition the same way they use their sight and hearing —as a valid sense and another way to process information.

I'll never forget this day when my daughter was about three. We were up early, headed to daycare. The light turned green, cars behind me honked, impatient and ready to go. But something inside me said: *No. Wait.* The lane next to me began to move, and seconds later a car ran the red light and slammed into another vehicle so hard it spun across the intersection. I hadn't seen it coming but my spirit knew. Another save.

But intuition doesn't only keep us from danger — sometimes it points us toward love and joy. Like the time a friend of mine randomly met a woman she thought was beautiful, but dismissed as potential for anything serious because she lived halfway across the country. I immediately told her that she was "the one". Years later I was dancing at their wedding. To this day Jasmine and Jasmine (yup, they even have the same name), remain one of my favorite love stories.

I could fill a whole book with stories like these — moments where intuition protected me, pushed me, or placed me exactly where I needed to be. But the bigger picture is this: intuition has always been our people's survival tool. As one African proverb says,

"Wisdom is like a baobab tree; no one individual can embrace it."

And when we look back, we see whole communities that turned intuition into liberation strategy.

The Maroons of Jamaica and Suriname were formerly enslaved Africans who used deep intuition, knowledge of the land, and spiritual practices to outsmart colonizers. They moved silently through forests, set up ambushes, and often credited their victories to ancestral guidance[16].

And then there's Sojourner Truth, a formerly enslaved woman who became a powerful abolitionist and women's rights activist. She often described hearing an inner, divine voice that guided her to freedom.

One day she literally just walked away from the New York farm where she was enslaved, carrying only her infant daughter Sophia. She went barefoot for miles, through woods and fields, following no map. She later said she felt God's presence every step of the way. When she finally reached the home of Isaac and Maria Van Wagenen, a Quaker couple, she asked if they would take her and her baby in. They did —

buying her freedom for twenty dollars. To trust that she would arrive at the door of people willing to risk punishment — and pay the equivalent of thousands of dollars for her freedom — required a faith that defied reason.

Sojourner later said, "I did not run away, I walked away by daylight, leaving the best of masters, kind mistresses, and a good home, for the Lord directed me."[17].

Her mission afterward — preaching and empowering others — was grounded in following that inner voice, even when it made no logical sense. That's what trusting intuition looks like: raw, terrifying, but powerful. Taking steps even when you can't see the path.

We have all had times where we had to trust a path we could not see.

I had doubts when I chose hairstyling as a career — especially after a quick Google search told me the average income was about $50,000 a year. (Note to self: maybe don't plan your whole future based on Google.) But within two years, I was making over $100,000 annually.

I was terrified when I published my first book. I'm naturally shy and I had a lot of doubts about being that open and vulnerable. That leap, though, opened doors to stages across the world — which is wild, considering how introverted I can be.

I second-guessed myself again and again when I felt the tug to return to school. It had been fifteen years since I earned my A.A., and staying in the career I knew — the one that paid the bills — felt far safer. I worried my brain might not still have "student mode," or that I'd end up overwhelmed and in tears halfway through the semester.

Still, I listened.

I returned to school, graduated with honors, and surprised myself with what was possible when I stopped talking myself out of the call.

And despite the success of my first book, I'm terrified to release this one. I've started and stopped countless times. Still, I keep going because of what I see happening in the world around me. I feel a need to speak up, speak out, and help us heal.

Here's the truth: when that voice calls, we must listen. Sometimes we have to get out of our way to receive the blessings God and the Universe has in store. When we tap into that universal source, we are guided toward a life far beyond our wildest dreams.

And honestly, my doubts are small compared to what our ancestors faced. The fear of going back to school is nothing compared to risking everything for freedom or being the first EVER to do something. Nat Turner spoke of visions, of the sun darkening and spirits urging him to act. His deep intuition became the spark for one of the most significant rebellions in U.S. history.

Bessie Coleman was the first Black woman to earn a pilot's license. Every American flight school denied her entry, but she trusted her calling to fly. She followed her instincts across the ocean to France, where she trained, earned her license, and came back to the U.S. determined to inspire others. She broke barriers in the sky that still inspire today [18].

Nat Turner led with rebellion and Bessie Coleman with innovation.

But they were guided by the same force: intuition, that deep knowing that whispers *"go"* even when logic says *"stay."*

So tell me: what is that voice asking of you right now?
What dream have you been tucking away?
What gift have you been too afraid to share?
What leap have you been waiting for "the right time" to take?

Guess what? There will NEVER be a perfect time — only the moment you decide to listen.

And when you do, you step into alignment with all the universe is waiting to give you.

*"To survive the trauma of racism,
we have had to become extraordinarily strong.
Strength, however, is not the same as wellness."*

— *Thema Bryant*

Chapter 3

Racial Battle Fatigue

Being Black in America requires a special kind of strength — one that comes at a cost. We carry the stress of being human alongside the weight of constant racial injustice.

The microaggressions.
The systemic inequities.
The constant need to prove, explain, brace, and endure.

This chronic exposure to racial stress has a name: **Racial Battle Fatigue.**

Racial Battle Fatigue (RBF), coined by Dr. William A. Smith, describes the psychological, emotional, and physical toll of constantly navigating racism. It's the exhaustion that accumulates from perpetual vigilance, coded insults, structural barriers, and the unspoken pressure to survive what others never have to consider. In short, it's what happens when being Black in America doesn't just shape your day — it reshapes your nervous system, your health, and your spirit.

Growing up, I didn't have language for it. I only noticed that I was treated differently than my white peers and even some family members. By the time I reached adulthood, that difference had settled into a kind of exhaustion that rest didn't fix.

Then, at thirty-seven, everything I thought my life would look like began to unravel.

Like many people, I had imagined a different future. I thought I would meet "the one" early. I pictured a Corey-and-Topanga kind of love. I imagined five kids, a strong marriage, lifelong friendships, excellent health, and a career that unfolded effortlessly. I assumed life would make sense.

I've been blessed — but it didn't work out that way.

At first, my husband and I seemed aligned — hard-working, family-oriented, building that "white picket fence" life. We bought a home, traveled the world with our kids, and sent our youngest to private school. From the outside, everything looked perfect. Inside the marriage, we were unraveling. After a decade together, it was no longer safe, loving, or healthy. Therapy couldn't fix it — and trust me, we tried.

What I didn't fully understand at the time was how much of that stress was racialized. My marriage was interracial, and racism didn't stop at the front door. His mother stopped speaking to me after we married — something my husband later told me he believed was because I am Black. A Confederate flag hung openly in the home of a close family member. I also overheard his friends use the N word in casual conversation — language they appeared unbothered by, but which landed as deeply disrespectful and harmful. When those moments required protection or accountability, I was left to navigate them alone. Over time, that lack of safety, on top of our marital issues, took a toll. Home — the place meant to offer refuge — became another space where my nervous system stayed on guard.

The stress began to show up in my body. My blood pressure climbed. My eyesight worsened. Panic attacks became daily. Depression made the days hard to get through. And layered on top of the marriage was the "double tax" so many Black women know too well: the expectation to stay strong and composed in a world that questions our competence, polices our tone, and dismisses our pain.

When I finally left, people called me "strong." I smiled and said thank you, but inside I was thinking: *Strong? Sis, I'm just trying to remember how to breathe without crying.*

Staying busy became my coping mechanism. Projects, certifications, degrees, remodeling, writing- the list goes on. Sometimes that drive took me to world stages. Other times it left me questioning my life choices. Because momentum can look like healing when it's really just survival in motion.

What I eventually realized was this: what I had been carrying wasn't just the result of individual hardship. It was the cumulative impact of long-term stress, shaped by race, environment, and early exposure to adversity.

That realization became the foundation of my academic work.

The Systems That Try To Break Us

Like so many of us, I survived because I learned how to adapt. But if I felt this pressure, millions of Black women have felt it too.

Too often, in every facet of life, we are expected to just endure. To take blow after blow and still get up smiling. Nowhere is that expectation more dangerous than in our healthcare system. Even in hospitals we are given less pain medication, often dismissed and treated as if we have some superhuman tolerance for pain.

The consequences are deadly.

Black women are three times more likely to die from pregnancy-related complications than white women, regardless of income or education [20]. Serena Williams — one of the most celebrated athletes in the world — nearly died after childbirth when her concerns were ignored [21]. Just recently I read about a Black physician, who after being dismissed and ignored, almost died giving birth in the hospital where she works.

Society is often its kindest to children and pregnant women. But even then, Black women are denied the same care, concern, and compassion as others.

Racism shows up *everywhere*.

Housing:

Homes in majority-Black neighborhoods are under-valued by an average of $48,000 per home, adding up to $156 billion in losses [22]. Meanwhile, Black families purchasing in white neighborhoods often pay more-charged extra in loans even with similar credit [23]. These practices lock us out of generational wealth while propping up white access to it.

Employment:

Résumés with Black-sounding names are still 50% less likely to get a callback than identical ones with white names [24]. That means an entire career can be blocked before it even starts — simply because of a name.

Education:

Black children are disciplined more harshly, labeled more quickly, and supported less often than their white peers — even in early childhood. Curiosity is mistaken for defiance, confidence for aggression, and need for help as lack of ability. Long before adulthood, many of us learn to stay on guard in places meant for learning.

Policing:

Modern policing in the United States traces its roots to slave patrols. This shows up today as over-policing, criminalization, and the constant need for vigilance simply to stay alive. Too often, seeking help risks escalation, violence, or death rather than safety.

Mental Health:

Black patients are less likely to receive accurate diagnoses, more likely to have symptoms minimized or misread, and often over-medicated rather than offered comprehensive, culturally responsive care.

Healthcare. Labor. Criminal Justice. Banking. Government. Policy. Tech. A.I.

The list doesn't end.

And the barriers don't disappear when we "make it." Racism still shows up in appraisals, hospital rooms, salary negotiations and everyday interactions. Then, when we speak on it, we're accused of "playing the victim" or "pulling the race card" by people who benefit from the very systems harming us.

But here's the part that gives me hope: we keep shattering ceilings, earning degrees, launching businesses, and leading innovation. The number of Black individuals earning master's degrees rose by 60% from 2000 to 2020 [25]. Black women, in particular, are the fastest-growing group of entrepreneurs in the U.S. [26].

Even our DNA carries resilience: research points to unique genetic strengths connected to African ancestry, such as lower rates of osteoporosis and stronger immune system markers [27].

What was meant to break us has only added to our strength. Still, chronic stress has an impact.

The Body Keeps Score

Whether it's divorce, the loss of a loved one, or navigating racism at work, chronic stress takes a physical toll. Our bodies absorb every blow — even the ones we think we've pushed through. That's why having healthy tools is essential.

When I was younger I numbed myself with things that would quiet the pain. But after crashing and burning more than once, I learned something important: **you can't outrun, outwork, or out-achieve unhealed pain.**

So finally, I stopped running and started to lean into practices that restored me.

I started working out consistently, eating raw foods and taking beetroot supplements (which significantly improve cardiovascular health) [28]. Within months, my blood pressure dropped and my eyesight improved so much that my optometrist told me I no longer needed glasses. (Though to be fair, when I'm driving down the freeway at night squinting at exit signs, I sometimes wonder if he was a little too optimistic.)

I leaned deeper into meditation and yoga to calm my nervous system, and as a result, my panic attacks almost completely stopped. In the last year, I've had only three. We'll go deeper in the next section on healing, but know this — it is okay to sometimes not be okay.

And healing doesn't mean you never fall apart.

It means you have tools to rebuild.

And that distinction is critical, because what happened to me isn't rare — it's patterned. The hypertension, the insomnia, the anxiety, the bone-deep exhaustion — these aren't individual failures. They are predictable outcomes of living in a body that is constantly asked to brace itself. As trauma researchers remind us, the body keeps the score.

Which brings us to the quiet, relentless stressors that rarely make headlines but shape our lives every single day.

The Impact of Daily Microaggressions

Police stops. Store surveillance. Slurs. Street harassment. Watching your child be the target of racism. These moments don't disappear when the incident ends — they settle in the nervous system, tightening the body for the "next blow."

I've watched an officer hit a U-turn, pull me over, and detain me for an hour trying to find a violation that wasn't there. My crime? Driving while Black.

I've walked down the street in a "nice" neighborhood only for a car full of white men to slow down, roll down their window, and yell, "Go back to Oakland!" My friends and I laughed that one off — "Well hey, how did they know?" — but the sting still lingered.

My daughter was only nine years old when she was followed around a pool and called the N-word. Needless to say, I ran to that pool barefoot and fists balled (I'm still working on evolving — don't judge me).

More recently, a friend of mine received her first bad review on Airbnb. A woman who seemed perfectly pleasant rented her back house for the night. Other than a few polite exchanges, nothing out of the ordinary happened. Days later, my friend got the notification: a one-star review. The comment was just two words—"Straight ni**ers."

Moments like these don't happen in isolation. They stack. And that's how hypervigilance gets wired in us. Because of this chronic exposure, we've learned to read the sideways glance, the sudden change of tone and the subtle exclusion that others pretend not to notice.

The same way my marriage pushed my body to the brink, racism pushes us collectively to the brink — only there's no option of leaving. You can divorce a partner; you cannot divorce racism. And our bodies absorb the cost of a system that refuses to see us fully human.

Culture, Media, and the Battle for Our Image

Black culture. Let's talk about it.

Mainstream America loves our culture—but often erases us from it. Things we've done for centuries were once labeled "ghetto" or "low-class," only to be rebranded as fresh and inventive when worn on white bodies.

Durags on Paris runways.

Cornrows renamed "boxer braids."

The same features they used to compare us to monkeys they spend billions to emulate.

And while our culture gets repackaged, our image gets distorted.

In the media, negative stereotypes dominate. Black men are often portrayed as gang members or criminals despite the fact that we make up only a fraction of crime rates. Black women are portrayed as ghetto single mothers on welfare even though the data shows otherwise. The stereotype was never rooted in truth; it was rooted in politics and propaganda.

Studies show that when Black people are reported on as suspects in the news, they are more likely to be shown in handcuffs, mugshots, or being physically restrained. White suspects, by contrast, are more often shown in neutral or flattering images, such as smiling family photos or a professional headshot. On social media, posts that link Black people disproportionately to crime overrepresent Black suspects by about 25% compared to actual arrest rates [30]. The double standard is obvious: white mass shooters are called "mentally ill," while Black children are tried as adults with no context or empathy.

These portrayals don't stay on screens. They shape how Black people are perceived and treated in classrooms, courtrooms, hospitals, and everyday interactions[31]. Over time, this constant misrepresentation becomes another source of psychological stress—forcing Black individuals to navigate a world that consumes their culture while denying their humanity.

Representation Matters

I cried when one of my hairstyles was featured in MunaLuchi Bridal, the largest bridal magazine for women of color. For once, a Black bride — with her natural curls — was centered. This was almost unheard of at the time.

For decades Black women have been pressured to straighten their hair to fit into white beauty standards. In my 20 years as a hairstylist and salon owner, I've witnessed this time and time again. Clients straighten their hair before an interview, wear a weave when they have a presentation at work, or avoid braids the entire time they are on probation so they don't get fired. This is why, in 2019, California became the first state to pass the CROWN Act. It banned hair discrimination, making it illegal to deny jobs, promotions, or opportunities because of natural hair or protective styles.[32]. Since then, several states have followed suit — but the law still hasn't been passed nationwide, and cultural bias against Black hair remains.

It's even ingrained in our own culture. I remember walking into a salon hoping to get hired in my early twenties, my hair in a big curly afro. The owner looked at me and said "Well you would be cute if you did something with that hair". I smiled and said "My hair is done".

Thankfully, things are changing. We are seeing diversity on magazine covers, natural hair campaigns, and more brands realizing that inclusion is not just a "trend" but a necessity. Social media has also given us power—we don't have to wait for traditional media to validate us anymore. Platforms like Instagram and TikTok (although they are in many ways problematic) allow Black women, in particular, to showcase our beauty, our families, and our joy on our own terms. When a young girl can scroll and see a bride who looks like her, a CEO rocking natural curls, or a dark-skinned model in a major fashion campaign, it chips away at the old narrative.

Once my daughter sent me a TikTok that said "my mama's business voice be killin' me, girl that is not the real you." I literally laughed out loud. And clearly I wasn't the only one entertained because it had over half a million likes. We get it because we've all code-switched to be acceptable.

Code-switching is often framed as professionalism or adaptability, but it's also another form of self-monitoring — one more way we learn to scan ourselves before others do. Still, the more we name it, laugh at it, and challenge it, the less power it holds. In the process we're rewriting the rules of what professionalism, intelligence, and respect actually look like.

Naming the Truth Is the Beginning of Healing

For so long, I believed I was "strong" because I could keep going. I swallowed pain, outran stress, and called it survival. But once I learned about *Racial Battle Fatigue*, everything clicked. Finally, there was language for what I had been carrying my whole life.

I've always prided myself on powering through pain — whether it was racism, heartbreak, or life falling apart. I grew up blazing my own trail because I didn't see one that fit me. Baldwin said, "The place in which I'll fit will not exist until I make it," and I've lived that truth. But I've also learned that forging ahead means nothing if I'm not tending to my mind, body, and spirit.

Our reality is undeniable:
We navigate a country built to exhaust us.
We endure systems designed to keep us out.
We carry a weight most couldn't handle.

But naming that truth is only the beginning. The deeper work is remembering that we are more than what tried to break us. We are what has always kept us alive. And when we lean into that legacy, our healing becomes a blueprint for those who will walk this path after us.

"We do not inherit the earth from our ancestors; we borrow it from our children."

— *Native American Proverb*

Chapter 4

Inheritance

When we think about inheritance, most of us picture what has been passed down from our ancestors—values, culture, memories, and lessons. But inheritance also moves forward. It's about what we pass on to those who come after us.

That raises an important question: what will our children inherit? Will it be healing or pain? Generational curses or fresh examples of how to break generational maladaptive patterns? Will they inherit our ability to rise, or the trauma we never took the time to heal?

Every generation has a choice—to pass down survival or transformation. This chapter is about choosing transformation.

But to move forward intentionally, we have to understand what we're already carrying. Before we can decide what to pass on, we must recognize what our ancestors have already given us. They've given us spiritual, cultural, intellectual, emotional, and physical gifts that continue to shape our lives today. When we learn how to access and nurture those gifts, they become tools for resilience, wellness, and generational change.

One of those tools is music.

The Neuroscience of Black Sound

Music rewires our bodies. For generations, music has been more than entertainment. It was survival, communication, and resistance. Spirituals, protest songs, and gospel music helped our ancestors process trauma and stay connected to hope.

Long before neuroscience had language for it, our bodies already knew.

Today, science is finally catching up. Researchers at Johns Hopkins University found that listening to music activates nearly every region of the brain—areas responsible for memory, emotional regulation, movement, and meaning. Music doesn't just pass through us; it organizes us. It helps the brain make sense of experience and restore balance when the nervous system has been overwhelmed [33].

Another review published in *Trends in Cognitive Sciences* found that music lowers blood pressure, heart rate, and cortisol—the hormone most closely associated with chronic stress. In other words, music calms the body's internal alarm system [34]. That's why a song can slow your breathing, soften your muscles, and offer relief for your entire body.

I lived this long before I understood it.

For years, I attended Wednesday night Bible study. But I would arrive an hour early just to sit and listen to the choir rehearse. Something about those voices would loosen something deep inside me. I left feeling lighter, steadier and more whole. I didn't have the language for it then, but my nervous system was being regulated in real time.

Science now confirms that this kind of regulation isn't accidental.

A 2015 study published in *The Lancet* analyzed data from more than 7,000 patients and found that listening to music before, during, or after surgery significantly reduced pain and sped up recovery. Music didn't just distract patients—it changed how their bodies processed pain altogether [35].

There's a story shared among researchers about a woman who believed so deeply in music's healing power that she requested it be played during her surgery. When her doctor refused, she found another surgeon willing to honor her request. The results were so remarkable that he began incorporating music into all of his procedures—and continues to do so to this day.

We see this truth echoed outside of hospitals too.

Former prisoners of war, kidnapping survivors, and people raised in abusive homes often recount the same thing: a song became their lifeline. Some mentally replayed hymns to survive isolation. Others clung to a single melody when they had nothing else to hold onto. Music gave structure to chaos, rhythm to fear, and meaning when their environment offered none. It reminded them—*I am still here.*

Sound is not just something we hear. It is something our bodies respond to, regulate with, and heal through. Melodies move molecules. Rhythm restores order. Harmony reminds the nervous system what safety feels like.

Songs like *Lift Every Voice and Sing* carried generations through the weight of injustice while holding onto hope

Sing a song full of the faith that the dark past has taught us,
Sing a song full of the hope that the present has brought us;
Facing the rising sun of our new day begun,
Let us march on till victory is won.

It's not just a hymn — it's an anthem of resilience, passed down like a sacred gift.

Think of the spirituals that carried coded messages of escape: *"Wade in the Water"* signaled enslaved people to move through rivers to avoid dogs and patrols. *"Follow the Drinking Gourd"* pointed to the Big Dipper— a map to freedom in the night sky.

Music became a language of survival, and it still grounds us today. Studies show that Black Americans consistently report higher levels of religious participation, prayer, and spiritual engagement than the general population. That spiritual connection, in all its forms, is one reason we've been able to keep hope alive through centuries of injustice.

Music isn't just art; it's inheritance. Alongside that spirit is our genius for invention.

Innovation In Our Blood

In 1519, William Horman said, "Necessity is the mother of invention." If anyone embodies that truth, it's us. One thing we will always do is make something out of nothing.

For me, that shows up in the kitchen. My family is from New Orleans, and cooking has always been a love language. I pride myself on cooking and hosting almost every holiday. But even on random weeks when the fridge looks empty, I can still pull together a full meal.

But it's not just about food.

Necessity has forced me to pivot more times than I can count. When my daughter was eight, I signed up to be the team mom for her competitive cheer squad. That meant gifts for every competition — and they were serious. We traveled across the country, winning some of the largest events in the world.

At the first competition, I bought custom jackets for each girl. Between the jackets and the customization, I spent almost $500. That was the last time I outsourced anything.

Instead, I bought a professional heat press and taught myself how to do it all in-house. Over the next decade, I made everything imaginable — jackets, shirts, robes, water bottles, makeup bags, blankets. I still make gifts for my son's soccer team, *Proud Mom* shirts for myself, and custom gear for my daughter, who's now eighteen.

That same resourcefulness showed up when I wanted to remodel my home but couldn't afford a contractor. What once helped me survive homelessness on a $1.75 bag of fries now taught me how to sand cabinets, paint walls, and install floors. It was the same skill: the ability to adapt.

This wasn't accidental. It was inherited.

Across generations, that same spirit has driven Black innovation. From jazz to hip hop, quilting to braiding, storytelling to entrepreneurship, we have always turned scarcity into abundance and struggle into brilliance.

That brilliance isn't just cultural — it's technological, scientific, and global. Black inventors and thinkers have shaped every aspect of modern life: the traffic light, the Super Soaker, the home security system, the clothes dryer, refrigerated trucks, the blood bank, open-heart surgery techniques, automatic elevator doors, the modern microphone, and even the first video game cartridge. That list is just the start.

Dr. Daniel Hale Williams, for example, became one of the first surgeons in the world to perform a successful open-heart surgery in 1893. When Black patients were turned away and Black doctors denied opportunities, he opened Provident Hospital in Chicago — the first

Black-owned hospital in America. He didn't just heal hearts; he opened doors for generations to come.

Then there's Katherine Johnson — the NASA mathematician whose calculations literally launched America into space. She was forced to walk all the way across campus, several times a day, just to use a "colored" restroom because none were allowed in her building. Yet her brilliance was undeniable. In 1962, John Glenn refused to fly until Katherine personally verified the numbers for his orbital mission.

For decades, her genius was buried under racism and sexism, but her work made history. Her story, brought to life in *Hidden Figures* (which I've watched at least ten times), proves that even when our brilliance is hidden, it still changes the world.

These aren't just "inventions." They're evidence that brilliance is our inheritance — passed down through every obstacle and every victory.

It's not an accident that many of these stories aren't taught in school. They are intentionally left out. Take Mary Beatrice Kenner, for example. She created the first sanitary napkin and drew investor interest until they discovered she was Black. After the rejection, she didn't stop. She went on to design the bathroom tissue holder, a back washer for showers, and a carrier attachment for walkers and wheelchairs. She eventually held five patents, despite constant barriers. Her story reminds us: inheritance isn't only what we receive. It's also what we create, persist through, and refuse to let die.

Her genius was undeniable. Me? Well, my inventions didn't exactly make history. Case in point- in middle school I thought I was getting my big break.

For a class project we were asked to create our own invention. I was always in trouble for staying up late reading, then waking up buried under a mountain of books. So I dreamed up a bookshelf on a lever — it would swing down when I needed a book and rise back up when I didn't. In my mind, this was the invention that was going to revolutionize bedrooms everywhere.

When it was my turn to present, I laid on the floor in front of the class and proudly demonstrated my invention, bracing myself for gasps and applause. Instead...literal silence. I looked over and saw a mix of confusion and disinterest on the students' faces. I got up slowly and awkwardly, my face burning as I walked back to my seat.

Clearly I wasn't going to be the next Mary Kenner.

So no, I didn't invent the next big thing — but I did learn that creativity isn't about perfection. It's about finding a way.

The Power of Community

The point is, we've *always* been creators. And our inheritance isn't just material — it's a mindset. It's the ability to see possibilities where others see obstacles. And we rarely do that alone.

From the manuscripts of Sankoré University in Timbuktu — where African scholars studied astronomy, law, and medicine centuries before Europe founded its first universities — to the brilliance that shows up in our HBCUs, barbershops, kitchens, churches, and living rooms- our creativity has always been nurtured in community.

Think of Mary McLeod Bethune, who in 1904 opened a school for Black girls with just $1.50 and a vision bigger than anyone around her could imagine. She went on to become a presidential advisor, shaping national policy at a time when most Black women weren't even allowed in the room. Or Dr. Charles Drew, who pioneered the modern blood bank, a discovery that has saved millions of lives. His work wasn't just scientific; it was revolutionary.

Even when we were denied access to mainstream systems, we built our own. Schools, hospitals, sororities, fraternities and churches weren't just institutions — they were lifelines. They provided education, safety, and belonging when the world refused to.

Our inheritance proves that creativity isn't just what we do; it's who we are. But inheritance is about more than individual brilliance — it's also about how we show up for each other.

The Nguni and Babemba peoples of Africa demonstrate this beautifully. When someone in the community makes a mistake, the people gather around them — not to shame, but to restore. They take turns naming that person's strengths and reminding them of their worth. The goal isn't punishment; it's healing.

That focus on community, empowerment, and upliftment followed us here. Enslaved Africans built churches, women's clubs, and mutual aid networks that pooled money, food, and care when formal systems shut us out. From the Black Panther Party's free breakfast programs for schoolchildren to the countless everyday ways we continue to look out for one another, collectivism has always been central to our survival.

We have also consistently stood alongside others fighting injustice. In the late 1970s, when disabled activists were protesting for equal access to education and public spaces, a group of them occupied a federal building for weeks. As they slept on cots and in wheelchairs, struggling to sustain the protest, they later named the Black Panther Party as a core part of their success. They credited them with bringing hot meals and support. One Panther explained it simply: "We're just trying to make the world a better place for everyone. That's what you're trying to do too — so why wouldn't we support you?"

There was no money exchanged, no recognition sought, and no incentive beyond doing what was right. That ethic of collective care — showing up for one another even when resources are scarce — remains one of our greatest inheritances.

The question now is: *What does it look like for you to continue that work?*

Giving Back: Legacy In Motion

You don't have to join a movement or march in the streets to give back. Sometimes carrying it forward means checking on a friend, pouring into your kids, mentoring someone, or using your gifts to make someone else's path lighter. That's how legacy moves through us.

Just the other day, a client told me about visiting her cousin in New Orleans shortly after Hurricane Katrina. Her cousin's home miraculously survived the storm. When they returned she opened her house to a neighbor who had lost everything. That neighbor had no money to give in return, so she offered what she could — joy, laughter, and the most incredible sweet potato pies.

That kind of love leaves an imprint. It taught me that abundance isn't always measured in dollars — sometimes it's measured in how deeply you show up for others. My grandma always said to whom much is given much is required. Basically meaning we have all been blessed at some point and we should all try to give back to others when we can. As kids she had us volunteer at shelters, she cooked and we passed out plates to the residents. I remember being reminded to be grateful for what I had- especially at times when I was embarrassed and resentful. I may have lived in a motel but at least we weren't in a shelter. We may not have had a kitchen, but at least we got to decide what we were going to eat each day. Maintaining gratitude in all situations was instilled in me.

I've carried that spirit with me. For more than a decade I've provided free haircuts and styles to unhoused men, women, and children in my community, often partnering with organizations that provide mobile showers, clothing, and meals. When my daughter was young she came to sweep and clean. Now, as an adult, she does hair and makeup for the participants. Sometimes we set up at veterans halls, community centers, Boys and Girls Clubs, or homeless shelters. Other times we work right on the street, next to encampments.

Once, I was cutting a man's hair when I noticed a long, thin cut running across his scalp, held together with metal staples. I can't work in anyone's hair if they have open wounds. So I sat down next to him and gently asked what happened. He told me he had just been discharged from the hospital, where he'd learned he had stage 4 brain cancer.

I hesitated and then asked if he planned on telling his family. He said no — that they wouldn't want to hear from him.

Something about that broke me. I told him that if he were my father, brother, or cousin, I would want to know. I would want the chance to say I loved him. To make amends. To sit with him and make sure he didn't walk through his last days alone.

We sat there in silence for a moment, the air thick with everything unspoken. Finally, he quietly said "Yeah, I think I'll give them a call".

Those are moments I will never forget. Still, seeing children living in shelters is the most painful for me. While I can't change their circumstances, I focus on what I can do. Many times their parents have much bigger worries than their hair. But a black child without their hair combed stands out. Braids, a press, locs or a twist out is a small way to give a child a sense of pride and normalcy, even in the middle of chaos. Plus, the chance to be pampered at one of your lowest moments can often be the first step toward healing. When we restore someone's sense of being seen and valued, even in small ways, we plant the seed that they are worth caring for — by others, and by themselves.

That belief has guided so much of my work, both behind the chair and beyond it. I've sponsored two children's education programs in Africa for the last 6 years, I host free workshops for young people of color throughout the States and I try my best to volunteer whenever possible.

I am far from alone. Across the country, ordinary people like myself are constantly stepping up with our time, resources, and love.

A 2012 study from Indiana University found that Black Americans donate a higher percentage of their income than other groups [36]. Recent research also shows that in 2022, organizations serving communities of color—where Black-serving organizations are included—received only 2.9% of total philanthropic dollars, highlighting both our generosity and the barriers to equitable support [37]. Despite the inequality we receive, we refuse to turn our back on others.

In ways both big and small, we give the love and support we should have received.

Legacy of Resistance

Our story of giving is only half the picture. We've also inherited a different kind of strength — the will to stand up, speak out, and fight back. Giving and resistance are both forms of love: one nurtures, the other protects.

We come from a lineage of fighters — people who refused to give up, who were forged in the fire, and who understood that we can do anything we set our minds to. That legacy of resilience has always fueled me.

For me, one of the places that fire shows up is in my love for books. I've said it before, but I'm obsessive about them. I've kept nearly every book I've owned since childhood, collecting literature the way some folks buy shoes or makeup. My living room is lined with floor-to-ceiling bookshelves, overflowing with stories — 98% of which I've read. Out of all of those, there are some that have changed my life, books that shook something loose in my soul.

The Autobiography of Assata Shakur was one. I remember staying up until 4 a.m. to finish it, unable to put it down. Assata was a member of the Black Panther Party and lived through the government's COINTELPRO program — a campaign that deliberately targeted and dismantled Black liberation movements [38].

Let's pause here. The Ku Klux Klan — an organization built entirely on hatred and violence — still exists to this day, has at times been classified as a religious organization, and has benefited from tax exemptions. Yet the Black Panther Party, which provided free breakfast programs, health clinics, and protection for Black neighborhoods, was labeled a national threat. Why? Because those in power understood our collective strength — and they've long profited from our division.

Anyway, back to Assata.

In 1973, she was pulled over on the New Jersey Turnpike. According to her autobiography, she stepped out of the car with her hands in the air — unarmed, surrendering — and was shot by state troopers. She collapsed on the pavement while the officers stood over her, watching, waiting for her to die.

But she didn't.

Instead of receiving care, she was arrested at the hospital, interrogated while sedated, and later charged with murder in a deeply flawed trial riddled with misconduct. Evidence was tampered with. Witnesses recanted. Still, she was convicted and sentenced to life in prison.

The state tried to silence her, to bury her spirit behind concrete and steel, but she refused to be broken. Even in captivity, she wrote, organized, and spoke truth to power. And in 1979, with the help of allies who believed in her innocence, she escaped from prison and eventually fled to Cuba, where she remained a political refugee until her death in 2025.

Her story is a reminder that even when caged, our people have never stopped resisting.

As Assata herself wrote: *"It is our duty to fight for our freedom. It is our duty to win. We must love each other and support each other. We have nothing to lose but our chains."*

The Backlash to Our Brilliance

History has shown that every time Black progress rises, there's a counterforce determined to push it back.

Look at Tulsa, Oklahoma — home to Black Wall Street, one of the most prosperous Black communities in American history. Black entrepreneurs, doctors, and educators built a thriving economic ecosystem in the early 1900s. Greenwood Avenue boasted more than 600 businesses, including banks, theaters, restaurants, newspapers, and even airplanes owned by Black residents [39]. It was a place that proved what we already knew: given access, resources, and community, we don't just survive — we thrive.

And that was exactly why it was destroyed. In 1921, white mobs, backed by law enforcement, looted, bombed, and burned the district to the ground, killing an estimated 300 people and leaving thousands homeless overnight[40]. The entire thriving community was erased from maps and history books for decades. Yet even in tragedy, the legacy of Black Wall Street lives on as a reminder that our genius has never been the issue — racism has. And still, that resilience — that refusal to be erased — is part of our inheritance too.

You can see it today. Black women, in particular, are the fastest-growing group of entrepreneurs in the U.S. [41], and Black-owned businesses contribute over $200 billion to the U.S. economy each year [42]. From Tulsa's own *Greenwood Rising* center, which now educates and honors that history, to the thriving wave of Black creators, CEOs, and innovators today — we continue to rebuild, reimagine, and resist.

Black Wall Street wasn't the end of the story — it was proof of what's possible, and our people have been writing new chapters ever since.

But as our communities built, the systems around us doubled down on control. Modern policing in this country didn't begin as a service to protect all citizens equally. Its roots go back to slave patrols, organized groups tasked with chasing down enslaved Africans who sought freedom and terrorizing the communities that resisted. After Emancipation, those same forces evolved into law enforcement that enforced Black Codes and Jim Crow laws — tools of racial control dressed up as justice [43]. This is why, even today, disproportionate arrests, stops, and killings of Black people don't feel like a glitch in the system. They are the system working exactly as it was designed. From Ferguson to George Floyd, Breonna Taylor, and countless other names we should never have had to learn, policing continues to remind us that survival often requires resistance.

But we come from Harriet Tubman's midnight missions, Ida B. Wells' fearless journalism, Fannie Lou Hamer's declaration that she was "sick and tired of being sick and tired," Malcolm X's fire, Angela Davis's intellect, and today's activists who continue the fight. We've resisted through rebellions, lawsuits, marches, art, comedy, and song.

Take the Montgomery Bus Boycott — it wasn't easy. People walked miles, shared rides, and sacrificed for over a year. But it worked. They brought a system to its knees not with violence, but by refusing to spend.

Fast forward to 2025. When Target pulled many Black-owned products and scaled back its diversity initiatives, the backlash was immediate — consumers pushed back, activists called for boycotts, and within weeks, Target lost over $12 billion in market value.

You can't appeal to the conscience of those that have none, but you can impact the bottom line. Economic resistance has always been one of our sharpest tools for accountability.

And let me be clear — this isn't about blaming white people as individuals. There are good people of every race, and countless White, Asian, and Hispanic allies have fought, bled, and even died alongside us for equality. What I'm talking about are the systems built to protect power, and the inhumane people who support it and benefit from it. You can't appeal to the morality of a structure that profits from oppression — you have to disrupt it.

In fact, my own family reminds me that legacy is complex. I'm mixed — my father is white, and his side has a long history of standing up to injustice, even when it didn't benefit them directly. My great-uncle marched in the Civil Rights Movement and came back with a broken nose — a proud reminder of the price we've paid for justice.

My grandfather, Raymond W. Ickes, earned his bachelor's, master's, and law degrees from the University of Chicago, then became an assistant U.S. attorney for the Southern District of New York. Later, he served in the Marine Corps, was wounded at Iwo Jima, and was awarded a Purple Heart and a Silver Star. After the war, he joined the Justice Department and helped gather evidence for the Nuremberg Trials — where top Nazis were prosecuted. He was known through his words and actions to be a fighter for social justice, equality and civil rights. In fact, he even landed on Richard Nixon's enemies list- which he responded to by saying "Well, that's the greatest honor I've received in a long time".

My great-uncle Harold Ickes — nicknamed "Harold the Great" in history books — served as Franklin D. Roosevelt's Secretary of Interior and was directly responsible for key desegregation efforts during the New Deal era, opening doors in places where they had long been locked shut.

I am proud of what my family has done. That legacy of resistance and justice is part of my inheritance too. Still, I walk through the world seen as a Black woman. And that means I have lived life through the lens of a Black woman — one who knows what it is to be stopped by police for no reason, to be underestimated, to be overlooked, and to carry the weight of stereotypes. My reality is shaped by both sides of my lineage: one rooted in privilege and resistance from within the system, and the other grounded in resilience, survival and ingenuity outside of it.

Together, they remind me that inheritance is never one-dimensional — it's layered. It's the fire of Harriet Tubman, the brilliance of Black Wall Street, the strength of my grandfather standing in a courtroom against Nazis, and the resilience of my grandmother who moved from the South and bought 3 homes, creating generational wealth against all odds.

Yes, we inherit struggle. But we also inherit strength and the strategies to push back, to create, and to thrive. Surveys showed Black communities report higher levels of hope and optimism compared to white Americans, despite facing harsher conditions [44]. That optimism is not accidental — it's survival. It's not naïve — it's defiance. It's the kind of hope that has carried us through slavery, Jim Crow, and every obstacle since. And it's why, no matter what we face, we keep moving forward.

When I think about my own life, the ways I've rebuilt from homelessness, heartbreak, and hardship, I know I didn't do it alone. I had the whispers of my ancestors, the lessons of my family, and the collective strength of a people who have never stopped creating beauty out of brokenness.

My family's story is just one example of a larger truth: every one of us carries an inheritance shaped by our ancestors, our environments, and the ways we learned to survive. That inheritance is not just a reminder of where we've been, but a blueprint for where we're going.

And now, the question becomes: How do we take all that we've carried — the trauma and the triumph — and actually move toward healing?

PART II

HEALING THE MIND

No one gets out of life unscathed.
Our wounds take different shapes —
abuse, depression, assault.
Racial trauma, the loss of a child,
a diagnosis that changes everything.

But pain is not a competition.
It is a call toward shared compassion,
a reminder that we are more alike in our aching
than we are different in our stories.

Healing is like the phoenix that rises from the ashes,

the butterfly that fights and struggles to break free of
the cocoon,
the seed that splits open underground,
never knowing it's reaching for sunlight until it
blooms.

In a world that could break us,
Choosing joy, choosing healing - is an act of resistance.

-Natasha Ickes

"Neurons that fire together, wire together."

— *Donald Hebb*

Chapter 5

What You Water Will Grow

"What you water will grow". Those words changed everything for me. The more I paid attention to the thoughts I fed myself daily — the quiet doubts, the old stories, the fears that weren't even mine — the more I realized my mind had been shaping my life long before I ever picked up a wellness book.

By the end of this section, you'll understand why your mind responds to stress, trauma, and repetition the way it does — and how to change those patterns. You'll learn the science behind belief, the power of your words, and a few simple practices that can shift your mental state in minutes. Healing your mind isn't about perfection; it's about awareness, choice, and small daily tools.

And that brings us to the truth I wish someone had told me sooner:

Your mind is not just a place where you think. It's a place where you create your reality.

To help you create the reality you want, this section introduces a five-part method — rooted in science, ancient wisdom, and lived experience — that breaks mental healing into clear, practical steps you can return to again and again.

Before We Begin

Healing the mind is not about mastering every tool at once — it's about learning yourself.

Each principle in this section offers a different doorway into clarity, peace, and self-awareness, but you're not meant to walk through all of them today.

Think of these principles as gentle invitations.
Choose one practice that speaks to you.
Try it, observe how it feels, and let it unfold at your pace.
Your mind doesn't need pressure — it needs space, curiosity, and compassion.

Healing isn't a race.
It's a remembering.

THE MIND LIBERATION FRAMEWORK™

Five principles to reclaim your mental freedom, rewire old patterns, and strengthen emotional resilience.

1. **The Science of Belief** — How thoughts shape physiology, behavior, and perception
2. **Be Still** — Calming the mind to regulate the nervous system
3. **Conscious Communication** — How words, media, and self-talk rewire the brain
4. **Healing Spaces** — The role of connection, therapy, and community in restoration
5. **The Power of Perspective** — Rewriting the stories that once held you back

Let's begin.

Principle 1: The Science of Belief

The mind is more powerful than most people realize. Every belief plants a seed, and the body grows in the direction of what we believe is possible. Thoughts can build or break us. They can keep us sick or help us heal.

One of the clearest examples comes from a famous orthopedic study: some patients had actual knee surgery; others were simply cut and stitched back up. No repair. No procedure. Just an incision.

Both groups healed the same[45].

Their brains believed they were repaired — and their bodies responded.

Another jaw-dropping example of this mind-body power comes from the 1950s, in the story of a man named Mr. Wright. Science books still talk about him, and every psychology student learns about him, because his case is one of the clearest (and strangest) examples of the placebo effect ever recorded.

Wright was bedridden with advanced cancer, his body riddled with tumors, and given only days to live.

His doctors offered him a brand-new "miracle drug" called Krebiozen. He believed in it so completely that within days his tumors shrank and he went from dying in bed to walking, laughing, and living again. For two months, he thrived.

Then he read news reports suggesting Krebiozen might not work. His belief collapsed — and within days, so did his health. His cancer came roaring back.

His doctor, desperate to help, conducted an experiment. He told Wright that a newly developed "superpurified" version of Krebiozen was available — and injected him with nothing more than sterile water. Once again, Wright's tumors shrank, his strength returned, and his hope rose. Not because of medicine, but because of belief.

When the American Medical Association officially announced that Krebiozen was completely ineffective, there was no saving Wright's faith. His cancer returned aggressively, and within weeks, he passed away [46].

Psychologists have studied this case for decades because it shows just how much power the mind has over the body. His belief didn't just lift his mood; it altered his physiology. His immune system responded as if the medicine were real.

Research shows this over and over again: belief can trigger endorphins to ease pain, dopamine to lift mood, and immune responses that fight disease. That's what scientists call the "placebo effect." I call it belief becoming biology [47].

For example, in one study involving Parkinson's patients, simply expecting medication caused their brains to release dopamine — the same chemical produced by the actual drug. Their expectation alone shifted their brain chemistry.

That's the wild part: our thoughts aren't just floating ideas. They send signals to the nervous system, hormones, and immune cells. Believing you're safe can calm your heart rate and steady your breath. Believing you're in danger — even when you're not — can spike cortisol and adrenaline until your body burns out.

So when I say heal your mind, heal your life — it's not poetic fluff. It's neuroscience. Your mindset can literally change your biology.

So how do you build a belief system that works *for* you, not against you?

It starts small. Beliefs aren't born fully formed — they're shaped through repetition, language, and the stories we tell ourselves every day. If you want different outcomes, you have to feed your mind different messages. That means noticing the thoughts that weaken you, interrupting them, and replacing them with ones that support who you're becoming.

These shifts matter because they change your internal chemistry. Neuroscience shows that repeated thoughts — especially those paired with emotion — form stronger neural pathways over time. In simple terms: what you practice thinking becomes what you believe, and what you believe shapes how your body responds.

Exercise: Belief Awareness

Noticing the thoughts that shape your body and behavior.

Step 1: Identify the Belief Loop

Write down one belief that keeps coming up for you lately.

Examples:

- "I'm too overwhelmed."
- "I always mess things up."
- "I never have enough time."
- "Good things don't last for me."

Your belief:

Step 2: Ask the Three Questions

Is this belief:

1. **True?**
2. **Helpful?**
3. **Aligned with who I'm becoming?**

Circle one for each. If you circle "no" more than once, this belief is ready to be rewritten.

Step 3: Track the Body Response

Where do you feel this belief physically?

- Chest
- Stomach
- Shoulders
- Back
- Throat
- Head
- Other: _____

Reflection:

What does this sensation tell me about how this belief affects my body?

Step 4: Rewrite the Belief

Choose a replacement belief that is believable *and* supportive.

Examples:

- "I'm learning to handle things differently."
- "I can take one step at a time."
- "I deserve ease."
- "I am capable of change."

New belief:

Step 5: Anchor It

Say it out loud once.
Notice how your body responds.

Reminder:
Belief becomes biology. The more you rehearse it, the more your brain rewires around it.

Principle 2: Be Still

So how do we quiet a mind that's always running the show?

Stillness.
Not the mountaintop, three-hour kind — the *I need five minutes to breathe before I lose it* kind.

Stillness isn't about emptying your mind or becoming someone who never gets overwhelmed. It's about giving your nervous system a break from constant activation. In a world built on urgency, stillness sends a signal the body rarely receives: *you are safe right now.*

When we slow down on purpose, the body begins to shift out of fight-or-flight and into regulation. Heart rate steadies. Breathing deepens. Stress hormones like cortisol decrease, while systems responsible for calm, focus, and repair come back online. Over time, these moments of pause retrain the brain to respond rather than react.

Research shows that regular practices of stillness — including meditation, breathwork, prayer, and intentional silence — can lower blood pressure, reduce inflammation, improve sleep and emotional regulation, and reduce symptoms of anxiety, depression, PTSD, and chronic stress[48]. Not by avoiding reality, but by changing how the body responds to it.

And stillness doesn't require perfection or long stretches of silence. It requires interruption — pausing long enough to step out of reactivity and return to regulation.

Stillness doesn't only happen on a cushion. It can look like:

- taking five slow breaths before responding
- Walking in nature
- sitting in silence instead of reaching for your phone
- praying, humming, or listening to calming sound
- resting your body without multitasking

- pausing long enough to notice what you're feeling

These small moments send a powerful message to the brain: *you are not in danger right now.*

For people who have spent years in survival mode, stillness can feel uncomfortable — even threatening — at first. That resistance doesn't mean you're doing it wrong. It often means your body has learned to associate motion with safety.

Stillness is how we teach it something new.

Knowing this doesn't make it easy. And I'll be honest: I'm still working on it. I often drive in silence, center myself before responding, and weave deep breathing into my day. But meditation is where I struggle to find consistency.

Here's why: when I first started, meditation felt like more work than putting together an IKEA bookshelf without the instructions. I'm really good at *doing* — not so great at *being*. It's not uncommon for me to wake up and decide to paint a room, rip up carpet, install new floors over a weekend, or teach myself how to sand cabinets on a random Sunday (never doing that one again).

But sit down for 20 minutes in silence?

Absolute torture.

As my coach once told me, the things we avoid are often the things we need the most. (And yes, there's even a book with that title — *The Obstacle Is the Way* by Ryan Holiday.) I believe them both- but that wisdom wasn't enough to get me meditating. What finally pushed me was two brutal nights of insomnia.

Now listen, I'm like a toddler when it comes to food and sleep — don't mess with either. But those nights, I couldn't sleep to save my life. I tossed, turned, prayed, stared at the ceiling, tried every trick I knew, and by 3 a.m. I was still wide awake. Then 6 a.m. came anyway — breakfast to make, kids to take to school, a full day in the salon on my feet with no lunch break, after-school sports, dinner, showers, dishes... you get the picture. By the second night, I was literally crying, begging God for relief.

That's when I finally gave meditation a real shot. At first, it was rough. Silence is loud.

But slowly, I found my rhythm. Now, I often meditate at night as a way to fall asleep. What used to take me hours of lying in the dark with racing thoughts now takes 10–20 minutes, max. And on my best days, I even start the morning with 10 minutes of meditation after yoga.

That's a win for me.

Stillness - in so many forms - is a tool to tap into our inner wisdom. And in a world that profits from our stress, choosing stillness is an act of rebellion.

Exercise:
Five-Minute Grounding Reset

A simple practice for calming
thoughts and healing your nervous system.

Step 1: Posture

Sit comfortably — on the floor, in a chair, or even lying in bed. Relax your jaw, soften your shoulders, unclench your hands.

Once you are comfortable, set a timer for 5 minutes (that way you won't keep checking the clock).

Step 2: Breath Pattern

Close your eyes and inhale through your nose for 4 seconds
Hold for 2 seconds
Exhale through your mouth for 6 seconds

Repeat 6 times.

Step 3: Notice Your Thoughts

They'll wander — that's normal. When they do, gently bring your attention back to your breath.

Step 4: End With Gratitude

When the timer goes off, take a moment to say thank you — for your body, your breath, or simply making it through the day.

That's it. Five minutes. You don't need a cushion, incense, or a mountain view. Just a willingness to pause. And over time, those pauses add up, rewiring your mind for more calm, clarity, and resilience.

Principle 3: Conscious Communication

Proverbs 18:21 reminds us, *"Life and death are in the power of the tongue."*

In Islam, the Prophet Muhammad taught, *"Speak good or remain silent,"* emphasizing the power of words to bring harm or healing.

In Buddhism, Right Speech is one of the steps on the Eightfold Path — a reminder that words shape suffering or liberation, both for ourselves and for others.

Across cultures and traditions, the same truth appears again and again.

The words we speak and hear shape our inner world. Long before science had language for it, African oral traditions, griots, and storytelling carried this wisdom forward.

Today, neuroscience shows that words don't just float in the air — they literally rewire the brain. Every phrase we repeat, whether positive or negative, leaves a mark on our neural pathways. That's why a single encouraging word can fuel a lifetime of confidence, and why constant exposure to criticism or negativity can weigh down even the strongest spirit.

So we have to be conscious of what we watch, listen to and talk about.

Like most people, I didn't always think about what I consumed. As a pre-teen and young adult, I watched whatever was popular, often without noticing how much negativity I was absorbing. Over time, I realized I wasn't just being entertained — I was being shaped. That awareness made me much more intentional.

But what we consume isn't just on a screen — it's also in our conversations.

Gossip, complaints, judgmental comments- all of it feeds the mind the same way negativity on TV does.

They are all hard habits to break, but it's possible. Owning a salon makes it even trickier — salons have traditionally been places where women let down their hair and talk about everything under the sun. But early on, I made a decision: in my salon, we don't tear people down. We don't speak death over each other. We don't use our words to harm.

Instead, we dream, we vent, we encourage and we lift each other up.

What I learned over the last 14 years as a salon owner is that conscious communication doesn't require perfection — it requires intention. Whether it's a workplace, a family, or a friend group, the same three principles apply:

1. **Set the tone.** Decide what kind of language belongs in the space — and what doesn't.
2. **Redirect without shaming.** Venting is allowed, but cruelty isn't. Honesty doesn't have to be harmful.
3. **Reinforce what you want to grow.** Speak life, possibility, and vision often enough that it becomes the norm.

When language changes, culture follows.

That commitment to positivity has created more than a workplace — it's created a sisterhood.

—

The brain literally rewires itself based on repeated thoughts and words — a process called neuroplasticity [49]. Rehearsing positive statements strengthens the pathways for confidence and resilience. Rehearsing negativity strengthens the pathways for fear, insecurity, and self-doubt.

And it doesn't stop at the brain. Words shift the entire body — heart rate, muscle tension, and hormone levels. Harsh language can spike cortisol. Kind words can increase oxytocin, the bonding hormone that makes you feel safe and connected [50].

Some call this the law of attraction. I call it spiritual physics. Your inner world influences your outer world.

And here's the truth: the stories you tell yourself ("I'll never get out of debt" vs. "I'm learning to manage my money") don't just reflect your mindset — they shape your behavior, your choices, and ultimately your outcomes.

That's why affirmations are a powerful tool to rewrite your inner script.

Affirmations aren't about pretending everything is perfect — they're about choosing the language you want your nervous system to repeat, what you want your body to believe and how you want your life to look.

Try speaking an affirmation out loud once in the morning and once before bed. Nothing dramatic — just a sentence that supports the version of you you're becoming:

- "I deserve peace."
- "My mind and body are healing."
- "I am safe."
- "I am becoming someone I'm proud of."
- "My life is expanding in ways I can't yet see."
- "I live in a friendly universe that wants to support me."

Small sentences = Big shifts.

Exercise:
Conscious Communication Audit

A simple practice to shift what you say, hear, and absorb.

This exercise helps you become aware of the language you use, the environments you sit in, and the voices you allow into your mind. No judgment — just awareness. Remember, anything you notice, you can change.

Step 1: Check Your Input

What's been feeding your mind lately?

Circle all that apply:

- TV shows filled with conflict, drama, or violence
- Messy social media pages
- Negative or biased news
- Music that drains your energy
- People who complain constantly

- Encouraging podcasts
- Documentaries / educational content
- Friends who speak life
- Books that inspire or teach
- Spiritual or grounding content

Reflection prompt:
What's one thing I'm consuming that drains me?
What's one thing that nourishes me?

Step 2: Notice Your Output

These questions help you observe your own language.

Check any that resonate:

- I vent or complain more than I speak solutions
- I downplay myself or talk negatively about my life
- I speak with hope and encouragement
- I catch myself oversharing or gossiping
- I uplift others with my words
- I apologize for emotions instead of expressing them

- I speak life over my goals, family, and community

Reflection prompt:
What patterns do I notice in the way I speak?

Step 3: Name Your Narrator

Every person has an inner voice. Sometimes it speaks truth. Sometimes it repeats old wounds.

Write down the **one sentence** your inner voice says the most lately.

Examples:

- "I'm overwhelmed."
- "I don't want to fail."
- "I'm figuring it out."
- "I'm doing better than I think."

Reflection prompt:
Is this voice protecting me, limiting me, or guiding me?

Step 4: Create Your Replacement Line

Choose a sentence that reflects where you're going, not where you've been.

Examples:

- "I'm capable and growing."
- "I can handle today."
- "My life is expanding."
- "I deserve peace and clarity."
- "I am learning new ways to be well."

Write yours here:

_____

Say it out loud once.
Notice how it feels in your body.

Step 5: Shift Your Environment

Choose **one** small change you'll make this week:

- Unfollow a draining page
- Limit news to 10 minutes
- Add one uplifting playlist
- Replace one show with a documentary
- Decline one conversation that feels heavy
- Spend time with someone who speaks life
- Speak one intentional compliment over yourself daily

Commitment:
This week, I will shift my mind by changing:

_____

Principle 4: Healing Spaces

One of the most powerful ways I learned to heal my mind was through therapy. Sitting down with someone who is licensed, trained, and has spent decades helping people move through the hardest moments of their lives can be life-changing.Unfortunately, only about 25% of Black people seek therapy compared to about 40% of White people [51]. And while things are shifting now, for a long time the Black community carried a heavy stigma around therapy. Part of that is cultural — but a lot of it is survival. For generations, therapy wasn't accessible to us, so we built our own systems of healing. The Black church became our counseling office, gospel music our release, and prayer circles our group therapy sessions. We leaned on each other because formal systems either excluded us or treated us as experiments instead of patients.

It's ironic to be less likely to receive therapy when we're often more likely to need it. About 65% of Black youth experience traumatic events compared to 30% of other groups, putting them at greater risk of developing PTSD [52]. And when trauma goes untreated, it doesn't just disappear — it can be passed down.

Researchers call this *intergenerational transmission of trauma*: the way stress responses, hypervigilance, and even unspoken pain can get carried from parents to children, shaping how entire families cope with the world [53]. That's why therapy isn't just about healing ourselves in the moment — it's about breaking cycles and creating space for future generations to thrive without carrying the same weight.

The truth is, many of us simply haven't had the luxury of sitting down to examine our feelings. When you're worried about where your next meal is coming from, drowning in debt, trying to survive a horrific boss, the only Black person in your law class, or dealing with daily microaggressions and chronic racism — therapy isn't the priority. Survival is.

I've dealt with depression on and off for most of my life. Sometimes it's faint in the background, other times I've been on my knees begging God for just one day of relief. And it wasn't until I finally had insurance, time, and the financial means that I was able to actually go to therapy. Once I did, I had breakthroughs I never thought possible. I shared things I swore I'd take to the grave, and I began to confront wounds from my past and patterns in my present so I could create a better future.

And here's the thing: those patterns weren't just about me. They were connected to something bigger. Racial Battle Fatigue doesn't just live in the headlines; it lives in our nervous systems, in our relationships, in our ability to feel safe enough to pause and breathe. Therapy gave me the space to name that and start unpacking it. Because there's real healing in having one hour a week where you don't have to be strong.

Beyond Therapy: Other Healing Spaces That Matter

Therapy changed my life — and I will always advocate for it — but it is *not* the only way to heal. Healing doesn't just happen in an office. It happens anywhere you feel safe enough to breathe, express, and be yourself without judgment.

Community is medicine. Connection is medicine. Creativity is medicine. Movement is medicine. For me, dance is medicine.

For some people, healing might come through:

- **A church or spiritual community** that feels grounding, not condemning
- **A dance class**, where your body shakes off stress you didn't even know you were carrying
- **A book club**, where you find people who think, question, and dream like you
- **A hiking group**, where nature becomes your therapist
- **A yoga or meditation class**, where your mind finally finds quiet
- **A creative space** — painting, writing, sewing, singing — where you release emotions through expression
- **A healing circle or support group**
- **A mentorship group**, especially for Black women
- **A culturally affirming community space** — the salon, a sisterhood group, the barbershop, a community garden
- **Volunteering**, where helping others helps you feel connected and purposeful

Healing happens in *any space that restores you.*

And for Black folks especially, healing often happens in places built on shared experience, cultural understanding, and collective strength.

Sometimes, the most powerful thing you can do for your mind is to find a space where you don't have to translate your pain or explain your existence.

What Makes a Space "Healing"?

It doesn't matter if it's therapy, church, dance class, or a circle of deeply honest friends — a healing space has three things:

- **Safety** — You can show up as yourself without fear.
- **Connection** — You feel seen, supported, or understood.
- **Restoration** — You leave feeling lighter than you came.

Anything that meets those three is a healing space.

Principle 5: The Power of Perspective

I vividly remember watching the movie *Pollyanna* as a child. The young star, a 10 year old girl, had every reason to be miserable after being orphaned, uprooted, and dropped into a life she didn't choose. Yet in every scenario, she found something to be grateful for. I remember thinking: *If she can find light in all that darkness, so can I.*

Growing up, that mindset shaped me.
If I got lost — I said it was a chance to explore.
If a relationship ended — I focused on what I learned.
If a door closed — I believed a better one was coming.

And while that mindset helped me stay hopeful, I eventually learned something important: **finding the good in a hard moment isn't the same as taking responsibility for changing your life.**

Gratitude can shift your perspective — but it doesn't replace action. And like many people, I sometimes used outside circumstances as an excuse for my own inaction.

That lesson clicked in my late teens when I read *Turn Your Life From a Problem Into a Solution* by Yehuda Berg. It showed me something I hadn't been ready to admit: as long as I kept blaming everything outside of me, I would stay stuck. I always had some degree of choice. Maybe not perfect options, maybe not options I loved — but options.

Once I accepted responsibility for my own decisions, everything changed. Within two years, I went from homeless and unemployed to a licensed cosmetologist on my way to making six figures.

Then, almost two decades later, I was going through a divorce. My ex-husband works in tech and has a healthy real estate portfolio. So I was terrified about the financial shift going into life as a single mom. Instead of staying stuck in blame — toward him, myself, or the marriage — I focused on what I *could* control.

I took a hard look at my finances and realized something many people don't talk about: six figures is a broad term. In a high-cost area, it doesn't always go as far as it sounds — especially when you're juggling education, housing, and the realities of everyday life. It wasn't stretching the way I needed it to.

So I went back to school. I started buying property. I accepted help when it was healthy. None of it was perfect, and none of it happened overnight, but each step shifted me from fear into action.

It's still a work in progress. But choosing to reframe uncertainty as an invitation to learn and adapt changed everything.

What I eventually realized is that perspective isn't about optimism — it's about agency. Research shows that people who believe they have some influence over their outcomes cope better with stress, recover more quickly from setbacks, and are more likely to take constructive action. This doesn't mean we control everything — especially in systems stacked against us — but it does mean how we interpret our circumstances shapes how long stress stays active in the body. Studies consistently show that when challenges are viewed as manageable rather than overwhelming, people experience lower levels of chronic stress, better emotional regulation, and greater resilience over time. Perspective doesn't erase pain — it influences how deeply the body absorbs it.

Reframing isn't pretending something painful didn't happen. It's choosing a new way forward- because stress becomes dangerous when it has nowhere to go.

I once heard someone say that a crisis is really a period of exploration — a doorway into growth. I believe that when life stops making sense, it's often an invitation to dig deeper and discover who you're becoming.

To make this tangible, let's end with a short exercise you can use the next time life throws you off balance..

Reframing Exercise:
The Shift Script

Reframing means choosing a perspective that empowers you instead of paralyzing you.

This exercise helps you move from reaction → reflection → reframing.

Grab a notebook, this gets deep.

Step 1: Name the Story

Write down the thought, belief, or situation that's weighing on you.

Examples:

- "I'm falling behind."
- "Nobody shows up for me."

- "I'm always struggling."

Be honest. No editing, no sugarcoating.

Step 2: Acknowledge the Truth of the Moment

What makes this thought feel real right now?
Write 1–2 sentences.

Example:
"I haven't hit the milestones I wanted. I'm tired. I'm overwhelmed."

This step honors your emotional reality without staying stuck in it.

Step 3: Challenge the Narrative

Gently ask yourself:

- Is this the complete story, or just the painful part?
- What else is true at the exact same time?

- What would someone who loves me say right now?

This opens the door to possibility.

Step 4: Write the Reframe

Now rewrite the story from a place of power, truth, and perspective.

Examples:

- "I'm not behind — I'm rebuilding with intention."
- "I'm learning how to ask for what I need."
- "I've survived every hard thing that was meant to break me. I can survive this too."

Make it honest, not cheesy. Real, not forced.

Step 5: Choose One Liberating Action

Reframing is powerful, but pairing it with action makes it transformational.

Ask yourself:
What's one small step I can take in the next 48 hours that aligns with my new perspective?

Examples:

- Journaling for 10 minutes
- Calling a supportive friend
- Signing up for a class
- Resting on purpose
- Setting a boundary
- Sending an email
- Decluttering one drawer
- Meditating for five minutes

Small actions build big momentum.

Step 6: Close With Gratitude for Your Growth

Write one sentence of appreciation for yourself:

- "I'm proud of myself for trying."
- "I'm grateful for my strength."
- "I'm learning to see myself with softer eyes."

This seals the shift.

Your Perspective Is Power

Reframing doesn't erase the pain — it expands the meaning. It helps you see the whole picture, not just the hardest part.

It's how you turn:

- crisis into clarity
- survival into strategy
- pain into purpose
- breakdowns into breakthroughs

PART III

HEALING THE BODY

Long before I learned the language of trauma,
my body spoke it fluently.
Migraine after migraine,
cramps that bent me in half,
a heart racing toward a finish line

I never agreed to run.

I ignored it

I hustled harder—
new goals, new projects, new distractions.

as if achievement could silence pain.
Work more. Sleep less.

Don't feel. Don't stop. Don't breathe.

Because stopping meant meeting
everything I'd pushed away.

So I ran. And ran. And ran.

Until one day, I didn't.

I breathed.
I softened.
I let myself be still long enough
to hear what my body had been saying
all along:

I can heal—if you let me.

-Natasha Ickes

"The task is not to control the body, but to listen to it."

— *Gabor Maté*

Chapter 6

When The Body Speaks

Across the African diaspora, healing the body was never separate from healing the mind, the spirit, or the community. Our ancestors practiced holistic health long before the term existed. In many African traditions, wellness meant tending to the whole person — physical, emotional, spiritual, and relational.

Traditional healers used herbs, roots, sunlight, steam, grounding rituals, drumming, dance, and breathwork long before Western medicine acknowledged the mind-body connection. Movement wasn't "exercise" — it was ceremony. Food wasn't just fuel — it was medicine. Sound wasn't entertainment — it was regulation, communication, and prayer.

These practices weren't alternatives.
They were the original frameworks of wellness.

And even after colonization attempted to strip them away, the wisdom survived — in our kitchens, in our churches, in our music, in the way we touch, tend, and care for each other. That lineage lives in you too, whether or not you were formally taught it.

This section is about reconnecting with that inheritance while also using what modern science teaches us about the body today.

Before We Begin

This section offers several practices for supporting your body, but you are *not* meant to do everything at the same time. You're not building a wellness bootcamp; you're building a relationship with your body.

Think of these pillars as invitations, not assignments.

- Choose one practice that resonates with you and start there.
- Let it meet you where you are.
- Grow at your own pace.

Healing is a lifelong journey — not a checklist.

My Breaking Point

I spent a lot of my life in survival mode- struggling with abandonment, instability and deep depression as a child. At 8 years old I started having migraines that left me incapacitated for hours.

By adulthood, survival had become my default mode. Homelessness, addiction, loss — each chapter taught my nervous system the same lesson: keep going, no matter the cost- achieve no matter what. But you can only run for so long.

Over time, everything started to catch up. I had migraines 4-5 days per week. My eyesight blurred. My blood pressure spiked. Panic attacks hit me weekly. Eventually I spent 48 hours with a heart monitor strapped to my chest trying to figure out what was going on.

One night, I felt my heart slam against my ribcage like it was trying to escape. My face was hot, sweat rolled down my forehead, and my breathing grew so shallow I thought I might pass out. Dizzy and light headed I stared at myself in the mirror — red, trembling, terrified. Convinced something was deeply wrong, I grabbed my keys and drove myself to the ER.

Thank God, hours later, the tests came back clear. No stroke. No heart attack. Just a doctor telling me, "Your blood pressure is extremely high and it sounds like you had a panic attack," before handing me a prescription for a blood pressure medication. On my way out of the hospital I threw it in the trash.

To be clear, not taking prescribed medication can have serious health consequences. This wasn't about ignoring a medical issue and putting myself at risk — it was about addressing it at the root. In my thirties, my body was going haywire and it was terrifying.

So I focused on healing my mind, body, and spirit through exercise, food and supplements. Within three months, my blood pressure dropped to the ideal range. My resting heart rate fell from the 90s into the 60s. My panic attacks almost completely disappeared. I no longer needed glasses. Piece by piece, my health began to return.

Modern medicine absolutely saves lives. I'm grateful it exists and use it when necessary. But for me, the first step was learning to give my body the tools it needed to heal itself.

The mind can create real healing when we give it the right conditions. Maybe for you it's not blood pressure — maybe you're struggling with insomnia, weight gain, heartburn or a body that just won't settle. Whatever form it takes, your body is listening to your mind. And as we just went over in the last section, that means you have more influence over your healing than you might realize.

After decades of research — and a whole lot of lived experience — I've learned that while healing is personal, there are four core pillars of physical health that almost everyone can benefit from. These are the foundations that help your body return to balance, restore energy, and begin repairing what stress has worn down.

These pillars echo ancient African approaches to healing — simple practices that reconnect the body to balance, safety, and strength.

Pillar 1: Nervous System Regulation

The nervous system is the bridge between what you *think* and what you *feel*. Stress in the mind shows up in the body, and tension in the body sends distress signals back to the mind. When the nervous system is dysregulated, both sides of that bridge suffer.

The nervous system operates in two main states: activation and rest. Activation — the sympathetic "fight, flight, or freeze" response — is designed to protect you in moments of danger. Your heart pounds, muscles tense, breath shortens, and your whole body shifts into survival mode.

That response can be lifesaving if you have to run from an attacker.

The problem is when we are chronically in a state of panic.

Bills, racism, microaggressions, trauma, unsafe relationships, and constant pressure can lock many of us into a state of ongoing alarm. And the body doesn't distinguish between a real threat and a perceived one — being chased by a lion feels the same as being disrespected in a meeting or scrolling through violent news.

This causes many of us to stay in fight-or-flight mode for days, weeks — sometimes even years [54].

This doesn't just wear you down emotionally; it can also damage your physical health. Chronic stress leads to your muscles staying almost constantly tense, which can lead to tension headaches, migraines, fibromyalgia, back pain and other body aches and pains. It can contribute to shortness of breath, increased asthma attacks, panic attacks and respiratory problems. Research has found a link between chronic stress and a higher risk of heart disease, stroke, diabetes, inflammation of the gut, higher levels of cortisol, constipation, diarrhea, sexual dysfunction, lower sperm count, infertility, herpes flare-ups, bloating, gas and acid reflux. It even shortens your telomeres, aging you at a cellular level [55].

Researchers have also found that stress may play a role in the onset or worsening of autoimmune conditions for 50–80% of people, and a large Swedish study published in *JAMA* found that individuals with stress-related disorders were significantly more likely to develop autoimmune disease than those without them [56]. In other words, stress isn't just "in your head." It leaves fingerprints on your immune system, hormones, and even your cells. There's an entire field of science — psychoneuroimmunology — dedicated to studying how stress and belief literally shape the body.

Elisabeth Kristof, a practitioner who teaches extensively about nervous system health and trauma-informed healing, explains it like this: when your system is stuck in alarm, your immune cells stay on high alert. Instead of resting, they're scanning for threats 24/7. And when there isn't a virus or infection to fight, your body can end up turning that attack inward — a pattern that can contribute to autoimmune issues and chronic illness.

This is why a regulated nervous system makes healing possible.

And this brings us to the simplest, most accessible tool we have — the breath.

Your breath is like a remote control for your nervous system — one of the only tools that lets you flip the switch from *alarm* back to *safety*. Slow, intentional breathing tells your brain, *"You're safe now. You can rest."* And once your brain believes that, your body follows.

The beginning of calming your nervous system is as simple as this: inhale, exhale, repeat.

Think about it: when your child is panicking, crying, and hysterical, what's the first thing you say to them? *"Calm down. Just breathe."* We know it instinctively, but most of us forget to practice it ourselves. (Funny how we'll remind our kids to breathe but go full fight or flight mode when someone cuts us off in traffic- I know that's not just me).

The truth is, breathing isn't just survival — it's medicine. And the best part? It's free, available 24/7, and doesn't come with a warning label listing 47 side effects.

There are many patterns of breathing that are proven to calm the nervous system:

- **Box Breathing** – Inhale for 4 counts, hold for 4 counts, exhale for 4 counts, hold again for 4 counts. (if you forget the pattern, just picture a box)

- **4-7-8 Breathing** – Inhale for 4, hold for 7, exhale for 8. It's like a natural sedative for the mind. Try it before bed and thank me later.
- **Humming Breath** – Inhale normally, then exhale with a gentle hum. Not only does it slow your breathing, but the vibration actually soothes your vagus nerve — the "chill out" switch for your body. Plus, it's kind of fun if you don't mind confusing the people around you.

My personal favorite is box breathing. I do it whenever it crosses my mind — in the car, before a meeting and especially on the sidelines of my son's soccer game. At a minimum, I practice two or three times a day. Within a few rounds, I can feel my shoulders drop, my jaw unclench, and my world slow down.

Box breathing isn't just some wellness trend. It's used by Navy SEALs, first responders, and elite athletes to stay calm in high-stress situations. Imagine being underwater, in combat, or running into a burning building — panic won't help you think clearly. Breathing does. If it works for them in life-or-death scenarios, it can definitely help you navigate traffic, deadlines, or a house full of kids on summer vacation.

Sound as Regulation

Sound is another powerful way to heal. It can be hearing your baby giggle (for years that sound brought me to tears), or a stranger playing the most beautiful notes you've ever heard in a random hotel lobby (it is enchanting). Sound reaches us in more ways than words.

Humming, chanting, and singing stimulate the vagus nerve. This nerve runs from your brainstem down through your neck, chest, and gut, touching almost every major organ along the way. When it's activated, your heart rate slows, your breath deepens, digestion improves, and your whole body gets the message [57]- *you're safe now.* That's why you feel calmer after singing out loud in the car, chanting in yoga, or even just humming softly to yourself. One 2020 randomized trial on Tibetan singing bowls found participants reported less tension, improved mood, and even reduced pain after just one session [58]. Other research links chanting and drumming with improved heart rate variability — a marker of nervous system resilience.

Of course, our ancestors knew this long before peer-reviewed journals confirmed it. From African drumming circles to spirituals sung in the fields, from gospel choirs to protest chants, sound has always been a tool for survival and resistance.

Other Ways to Regulate the Nervous System

Breath and sound are just the beginning. Your body also responds to:

- **Cold exposure** *(a splash of cold water, a cool shower)*
  Brief cold stimulates the vagus nerve, reduces inflammation, increases dopamine for hours and improves circulation[59].
- **Rhythmic movement** *(walking, dancing, rocking)*
  Repetitive motion signals predictability and safety to the nervous system, helping release stored tension and restore regulation.
- **Grounding** *(touching the earth, weighted blankets, laying on the floor)*
  The Earth carries a natural negative charge. When bare skin makes direct contact with the

ground—soil, grass, or sand—electrons can transfer from the Earth into the body. Research suggests this connection may help neutralize inflammation, lower stress hormones, improve heart rate variability, and stabilize the body's electrical systems[60].

- **Gentle stretching** (*especially slow neck and shoulder release*)
  These areas hold stress from prolonged vigilance; slow movement helps unwind the body without triggering alarm.
- **Touch** (*hugs, massage, pressure on the sternum or shoulders*)
  Safe, intentional touch releases calming neurochemicals that counteract fear and strengthen the body's sense of connection.

These practices tell your system, "You are safe." And when your body believes you're safe, it can finally begin to heal.

Your body has been speaking to you for years. What might happen if you started listening?

Pillar 2: Nourishment & Fuel

We've all heard the saying, *"You are what you eat."* Depending on the day, that can feel inspiring — or like a personal attack. And honestly, in America, nourishing yourself isn't always simple. Even our fruits and vegetables are often covered in chemicals, our cereals contain additives banned in other countries, and a lot of our meat is pumped with hormones and antibiotics we were never meant to digest.

So if you've ever felt confused or overwhelmed by the food system — trust me, you're not alone.

I grew up in a vegetarian household, but I was given the freedom to eat whatever I wanted. And I *did*. I was a carnivore through and through. Then, as I got older, I started learning more — reading books like *Fast Food Nation*, researching how our food is processed, and discovering things I wish I could un-know.

I won't gross you out with every detail, but here's one example. Dairy cows are repeatedly and artificially impregnated so they'll continue producing milk. But their bodies aren't meant to be kept in a near-constant cycle of pregnancy. Over time, many develop painful infections in their udders. That infection can lead to pus cells ending up in the milk — and yes, there are legally allowable limits for that in the milk sold at grocery stores[61].

There are audio recordings of mother cows crying out as their newborn calves are taken from them — the males often killed and sold for veal, the females raised to become dairy cows themselves. And when a cow becomes too weak or sick to stand, she can collapse from exhaustion or illness. I've seen footage of workers using machinery to lift or drag those animals away for slaughter. That same cow, once she's deemed "used up," becomes someone's hamburger.

And "free-range"? I used to picture chickens living their best life — sunshine, grass, the whole farm-to-table fantasy. The reality is very different. In most commercial operations, "free-range" simply means they aren't kept in cages. Instead, thousands of birds are crowded together on the floor of a warehouse, often with no windows and very little light. Technically, there might be a small door somewhere, but most birds will never reach it or even realize it exists[62].

I could keep going but you get the point. And I don't share any of this to shame you or police your plate — your choices are your own. My intention is simply to encourage awareness. Because the truth is, we can't expect to eat unhealthy, stressed, or overly processed foods every day and somehow become the healthiest version of ourselves. Plus, where I can, I want to stay away from the inhumanity and torture that is our meat industry.

The more I learned the more I started cutting things out — first milk and pork, then other foods that just didn't feel right for my body anymore.

Eventually I became 98% vegan (I will still eat the occasional cookie), but even that required another layer of honesty. Just because something is plant-based doesn't mean it's healthy. A lot of the fake meats I leaned on initially, were full of chemicals and inflammatory oils. Now, I still enjoy them occasion-ally, but most days I try to focus on whole grains, vegetables, fruits, nuts, seeds, and legumes. People always ask if I get tired of vegetables — but there are *hundreds* more types of plants than kinds of meat. My options expanded, not shrank.

Here's why this matters:

Food influences every major system in your body.

- **Your gut** houses over 70% of your immune system. What you eat feeds either inflammation or healing.
- **Your brain** relies on nutrients to regulate mood, memory, and focus — deficiencies in magnesium, omega-3s, B vitamins, or amino acids are linked to anxiety and depression.
- **Your hormones** are built from the fats and proteins you consume — which is why processed oils and ultra-processed foods can cause imbalance.
- **Your energy levels** depend on blood sugar stability — roller-coaster spikes from sugary or processed foods create fatigue, irritability, and cravings.

And here's a big one:

Chronic inflammation — often triggered by poor diet — is linked to heart disease, diabetes, high blood pressure, autoimmune conditions, and even certain cancers.

This isn't about labeling foods "good" or "bad." It's about understanding that your body is always communicating. When you're bloated, sluggish, breaking out, or crashing every afternoon, that's data. When you feel energized, clear-headed, and stable, that's data too.

So here are a few questions to help you tune in:

- What foods give you energy instead of draining it?
- What meals make your mood feel lighter?
- What foods leave your body inflamed, bloated, or uncomfortable?
- Where can you add more color — greens, reds, purples, oranges — instead of removing things?

Your body doesn't need perfection.

It needs consistency, awareness, and nourishment that supports the life you're trying to build.

Pillar 3: Rest & Recovery

I'm like a child when it comes to sleep — I need a full 8–10 hours. I always admire people who function off five, but that has never been my ministry. When I wake up, I'm on my feet for 12–15 hours straight, so when I lie down, I need real rest. And the truth is, far too many people — and I'll just say it plainly — especially Black women, are so busy carrying everyone else that our own rest becomes the first sacrifice. We're everything to everyone, and the only quiet moments we get are when the whole house is finally asleep. So we stay up scrolling, reading, thinking... choosing solitude over sleep, even though our bodies are begging for both.

But here's the thing: sleep isn't optional. It's biological maintenance and the time when the body repairs what life has broken down.

During deep sleep, your brain clears toxins, your cells regenerate, your immune system strengthens, and your nervous system resets itself. Chronic sleep loss does the opposite — it raises cortisol, disrupts appetite and stress hormones, weakens immunity, increases inflammation, and significantly raises the risk of anxiety and depression.

Research shows that getting fewer than 6 hours of sleep per night is linked with higher levels of psychological distress, impaired cognitive functioning, and increased risk for cardiometabolic disease [63]. Another study found that chronic sleep deprivation reduces the brain's ability to clear beta-amyloid — a protein associated with Alzheimer's disease [64].

While it's an extreme example, there *is* a real disorder — fatal familial insomnia — where the brain loses the ability to sleep and the body literally shuts down over time. We cannot survive without rest.

And rest isn't just sleep. We need:

- **Physical rest** to release tension.
- **Mental rest** from constant decision-making.
- **Sensory rest** from screens and noise.
- **Emotional rest** from being "the strong one."

When these forms of rest are neglected, the body sounds alarms — headaches, irritability, inflammation, exhaustion — long before we realize what's happening.

Recovery is not a luxury; it's a requirement. Your body cannot repair under constant pressure, and you cannot heal in survival mode.

Pillar 4: Movement & Flow

We've all seen it.

Two people in their seventies. One barely moves, lives in constant pain, and talks endlessly about what their body "used to" do. The other is laughing, traveling, dancing, flirting, hiking — often with more energy than people half their age.

The difference usually isn't genetics or luck. It's movement.

It's critical that we move our bodies. Intentional movement shifts stuck energy, helps us process stress, and supports every system in the body. Many modern Western diseases are linked to diet and a sedentary lifestyle, and movement is one of the most accessible tools we have for prevention and healing. Physical activity regulates the nervous system — releasing tension stored in muscles, lowering stress hormones, and boosting mood-lifting chemicals like endorphins and dopamine.

Here's the good news though. You don't have to be in the gym at 5am or start running marathons. You just need something that moves *your* body and feels good to *you.*

My parents modeled this beautifully. My mom ran marathons for years. She trained in the hills — running, hiking, whatever kept her connected to her body. One Sunday we were on a trail we visited often and saw a sign that said: Caution: Mountain Lion Sighting. I paused, but she shrugged and kept going. A few months later we returned and the sign had changed to: Mountain Lion Habitat. She was unfazed but I turned right around and went back to the car. Because while I value cardio, I value my life even more.

My father was just as committed. He was a bodybuilder, ex-military, and has trained his entire life. At the time I'm writing this, he is 80 years old and does **1,000 sit-ups and three hikes every day.** (No, that's not a typo.) He even met his girlfriend — the woman he describes as his soulmate — on one of his hikes. She's 90. They're in better shape than people half their age.

And my maternal grandmother? She was a whole inspiration in her own right. I grew up watching her in the living room doing those iconic 80s workout tapes — the ones with the neon leotards, ankle warmers, and enough upbeat music to power a small city. Later, she graduated to power-walking outside like it was her Olympic sport. She used to park at the mall and walk the entire outside perimeter before even stepping inside. And up until age 89, she still took the stairs everywhere she went — a habit she passed on to me.

So movement was modeled early for me, not as punishment or as a means to "look a certain way", but as a lifestyle. And I've made it my own. Yes, when I increased my cardio and people finally stopped asking if I was pregnant (my youngest was seven — Jesus be a fence), I was thrilled. But more importantly, movement makes me feel alive. It clears my mind, boosts my mood, and lets me *exhale*.

My absolute favorite is West African dance. The first time I went was because a friend invited me to a class. And although I'm shy and had zero prior experience, I thought, *why not?* I was clearly the newbie — always a half step behind everyone else, stepping left when we were supposed to go right, trying to keep up while silently praying no one was watching me. The truth is I should have been hiding in the back. Instead, I had the nerve to be in the second row. I figured if I'm lost up here with a clear view then I don't stand a chance in the back of the room. And even though I was embarrassed, something in me lit up. I couldn't fully explain it. Something about the live drummers, my incredible teacher Naby, and a room full of people moving in rhythm — all feels like therapy.

Rhythmic movement — like walking, dancing, rocking, or drumming — has been shown to soothe the limbic system and support trauma recovery. Flowstate activities (anything that fully absorbs your attention) lowers anxiety, sharpens focus, and creates emotional spaciousness.

And because you know I'm a little obsessive, once I fell in love with it, I was all in. I started going three times a week and trained so hard I wound up with a stress fracture that took five months to heal. Then I went right back and haven't stopped since. I can now keep up, often lead the dances and I even danced in a parade where our group won first place. Not bad for someone who hadn't taken a dance class since I was eight.

The point is this:

Try things. Explore. Play. Find what lights you up.

Take yoga for example. When most people think of yoga, they picture thin white women in stretch pants. While that's certainly part of the demographic today, yoga didn't begin in glossy studios or on Instagram. It originated in Black and brown spaces across ancient civilizations.

The most widely known roots trace back to India over 5,000 years ago, where yoga was created as a practice to unify mind, body, and spirit. Some scholars also point to Africa — specifically ancient Kemet (Egypt) — where temple carvings and hieroglyphs depict figures in postures strikingly similar to modern yoga poses[65]. These images suggest that yoga-like movement and meditative practices may have existed within African spiritual traditions long before the West commercialized yoga as fitness.

Whether you look at the Indus Valley or the Nile Valley, the message is the same: yoga was never about aesthetics. It was about presence, breath, discipline, and healing — and that belongs to all of us, in every body.

Choose One

As you finish this section, pause and ask yourself:

- Which tool felt most supportive for where I am right now?
- Which practice do I want to try this week?
- Which one feels too heavy, too much, or not right for me at this moment?

Your body will guide you. Your job is simply to listen.

PART IV

HEALING
THE SPIRIT

Energy doesn't die.
It transforms.
Switches form like a master of disguise.
One lifetime you're flying through open sky,
the next you're here—
learning heartbreak, courage, laughter, survival.

But we get distracted by the visible.
We think the body is the whole story.
We forget the spirit keeps receipts.

And when life hits hard—
the kind of hit that drops you to your knees—
that's when the soul starts whispering,
Come home to yourself.

Healing the spirit isn't soft or optional.
It's rebellion.
It's resistance.
It's choosing to rise
when everything tried to fold you.

Talking to God.
Calling your power back.
Listening to the ancestors humming in your chest.
Breathing until your heartbeat becomes a prayer.

Knowing that healing isn't about becoming new—
it's about remembering
you were never broken to begin with.

-Natasha Ickes

"Not everything that is real can be explained"

— *Carl Jung*

Chapter 7

When Spirit Speaks

Spirituality has always been woven into the DNA of African cultures — long before colonization, Christianity, or Western religion shaped what we were "allowed" to believe. Across the continent, spiritual traditions were diverse, but most shared a common foundation: the belief that everything is alive with spirit.

This worldview is called animism — the belief that places, objects and creatures all possess a distinct spiritual essence. It is the understanding that all things carry their own energy and intention. The land is alive. Water is alive. Trees, animals, ancestors, music, dreams — all animated with meaning. Nothing is just "there." It is all connected.

Therefore, God isn't distant or contained in one building. Spirit speaks through dreams, intuition, music, nature, elders, ritual, and community. It is a sophisticated spiritual ecology.

In Akan traditions, ancestors remain active guides, offering protection and counsel.

In many Central and West African practices, drumming, chanting, dance, and rhythm aren't performances — they are prayers, portals, and communication with the unseen.

In Yoruba tradition, people honor the Orishas — divine forces connected to nature, wisdom, justice, creation, and healing.

Among the Dagara people of Burkina Faso, each person is born with a unique spiritual purpose and elemental energy — fire, water, earth, mineral, or nature — shaping how they heal and how they serve.

In Kongo cosmology, there is no hard line between the living and the ancestral realm; the spiritual world mirrors ours, and communication flows both ways.

These traditions teach something powerful: Life is interconnected. Spirit moves through everything. And healing isn't individual — it's communal, ancestral, and embodied.

Colonialism tried to sever these practices from us —
labeling them evil, primitive, or dangerous. But our
spirituality never died. It adapted. It hid in plain sight.
It traveled with us across oceans and generations. It
whispered through our grandmothers' prayers, our
intuition, our dreams, our music, and the small rituals
of protection, cleansing, and blessing that survived
even when the language around them didn't.

One of the things that amazes me is that even
without being formally taught these traditions, many
of us have always been instinctively drawn to their
core principles.

A belief that everything is connected.
A sense that the natural world is alive and responsive.
An inner knowing that Spirit speaks in more ways
than one.

I was one of those children.

For me, connecting with Spirit was never optional —
it feels like something woven into my DNA. I've
always been drawn to the unseen, the intuitive, the
energetic. I talk to my plants. I feel the energy in a
room before anyone speaks. I search for depth and

meaning in everything. And I deeply feel that all things are interconnected.

As a child it started with traditional religious exposure- which I loved. Church felt like home. It settled my spirit in a way nothing else could, especially given the deep depression I began battling at an early age. But even then, I questioned everything. We were taught that when someone dies they go to heaven or hell. I didn't believe in a traditional hell and wasn't sure about the way heaven was depicted.

For a long time, these questions lived safely in my mind.

That changed when my grandfather passed away.

Shortly after he died, I was walking upstairs in my grandmother's house. As I approached the kitchen and glanced to my right, I froze. At the bottom of the stairs stood my grandfather. Not translucent, not floating, not ghostly — **solid**. As real as you or me.

I stared, certain of what I was seeing and completely confused about how it was possible. Then I did what any terrified child would do: I turned and ran. When

I finally crept back and peeked down the stairs, he was gone.

That moment cracked my world open.

And it didn't end there. After that, he made his presence known — lights flickering, TVs turning on and off, the dog growling at something we couldn't see. A friend once told me, "I'm not coming back to your house... you have ghosts." I laughed and said, "Don't worry. He's friendly."

But one moment I'll never forget: I was downstairs with my cousin Noel. We were relaxing and talking with the radio playing quietly in the background. Suddenly, the stereo blasted to full volume — and neither of us was anywhere near it. We stared at each other wide-eyed. I shrugged, "That's just grandpa." The moment that left my lips, the volume jumped to *maximum*. We screamed, ran up the stairs, and didn't look back. Those were the same stairs he first appeared on after he passed.

From there my spiritual curiosity only grew. As a teenager, I took a 40-minute bus and a 10-minute walk every week to attend church on my own. I read the Qur'an, studied Kabbalah, took a world religions class, and built my intuition — a gift I didn't fully understand but felt deeply.

Usually these warnings show up as an intense sense of knowing. Sometimes they're quiet. Sometimes they're urgent.

Like the time I warned my friend René for weeks not to go out on a specific day. He had witnessed my intuition enough times to trust it, so he stayed home. At least until around 11:30 that night, when he decided to run to the store for something quick and figured the danger had passed.

It hadn't.

He ended up sprinting for his life after a mistaken-identity incident that easily could've killed him. I picked him up hiding behind a truck, shaken but alive.

Another time I called my brother Jesse out of the blue and told him, *"Do not drink and drive tonight."* - something I had never done. I could hear his friends laughing in the background, but I repeated it anyway, telling him I didn't feel like anyone was going to get hurt — just that *he* shouldn't do it.

Less than an hour later, he called me back. He'd gotten pulled over for exactly that.

Once, I called my friend Brandon (someone I only spoke to a few times a year) with a sudden sense of fear, asking him to warn a mutual friend not to go out that night. The warning was actually meant for Brandon — my call woke him just in time to realize his coworker was trying to set him up and lure him somewhere unsafe. He didn't go.

Other times the warnings came in dreams.

I dreamed — twice — that my son would almost be hit by a car. Both times, the exact scenarios played out in real life, but just like in the dream, he survived. Thankfully I'd warned my entire family when I had the dreams and they were on high alert.

And then there were dreams that were heavier. Repeated. Vivid. The kind that cling to your spirit long after you wake. I had a dream over and over again, in which I was murdered. I would wake up in a panic, heart beating fast, terrified. I told my best friend and husband that some nights I was scared to go to sleep. I didn't understand it until a month later, when I learned my ex-boyfriend had been killed. The dream *was about him.* When I described it to his sister (down to what the killer was wearing), she confirmed that I dreamt of details only she and the police knew. That was the moment I realized my intuition wasn't just "a feeling." It was a bridge.

Years later, Ayahuasca cracked that bridge wide open.

I spent three days in the Peruvian mountains with traditional shamans. My ancestors came. The plants spoke. I asked questions and got answers — some comforting, some challenging, all transformative. Several days after the ceremonies, I visited Machu Picchu. During the tour we passed a quiet, unassuming area — and I froze. I had dreamed about this place years earlier. Now I wondered how I dreamed so clearly about a place I had never been.

Hours later, the truth clicked:
I had been there before. Just not in *this* life.

I have only told a handful of people because I didn't want to be dismissed or judged. But reincarnation isn't some fringe idea. There are thousands of documented cases. And deep down, I think many of us have felt that sense of having lived more than once.

Why am I sharing all of this?

Because the world is bigger — wider, deeper, more layered — than what we see.
Because every one of us has spiritual gifts, whether we acknowledge them or not.
Because intuition, dreams, energy, ancestors, signs — none of this is random.
Some people are clairvoyant.
Some are empaths.
Some feel God in nature.
Some hear their intuition like a whisper.
Some see signs in dreams or numbers or synchronicities.

All of it is valid.
All of it is holy.

I believe intuition is the piece of God we each carry — the inner knowing we weren't taught but somehow remember. And I believe spiritual connection is essential to healing. What it looks like is entirely personal: prayer, meditation, church, yoga, tarot, ancestral work, studying Animism, journaling, dance, singing, energy healing, time in nature, chanting, stillness.

There is no wrong door to the divine. There are, however, ways to nudge that door open— gently, consistently and intentionally.

So let me tell you a story.

Not long ago, I attended a conference out of town. Right as I was leaving the house, I felt a nudge to grab a small pink crystal shaped like a heart. No plan, no reason — just intuition. I've learned not to argue with that voice, so I slid it into my pocket and went on my way.

When we arrived, we were placed into small groups for an exercise called "heart work." The facilitator displayed a pink heart on the screen and said, "Grab anything you have that represents this — even a coin — because you'll be passing it around as you share." I reached into my pocket and pulled out the crystal. My whole group stared at me like I had performed a magic trick.

"How did you know we'd need that?" someone asked.

"I didn't," I responded.

When the first woman on my right held the crystal, she shared that she had been diagnosed with glioblastoma 13 months earlier and had been given 14 months to live. As she spoke, my chest tightened. But what struck me wasn't just her story — it was *her*. The topic was heavy but Amanda was absolutely hilarious and full of life. She cracked jokes, made us laugh, and also made me cry. My spirit connected to hers immediately and I knew I made a friend.

Later, during the break, I pulled her aside. I told her that on every trip, I bring a book to read, and this time I happened to bring *The Light Between Us* by Laura Lynne Jackson — a book about intuition, mediumship, and life after death. I told her I wasn't sure why, but I felt called to give it to her if she was open to it.

She said yes.

What I didn't know was that that book would become a lifeline for her — not because it cured her illness, but because it shifted her fear, reframed her relationship with death, and helped her feel held by something bigger than this moment. Today she is a long-term survivor, and we are still in touch. In fact, just a few weeks ago she went to a book signing by Laura Lynn Jackson and shipped me my own signed copy of her book.

I share this because none of it was an "accident."
Not the conference.
Not the crystal.
Not the book I tossed into my suitcase.
Not the two of us sitting in the same small group in a room full of hundreds.

That's how Spirit moves — quietly, subtly, through whispers, nudges, impulses, and timing you couldn't orchestrate even if you tried.

And here's the part where this becomes about *you*:

Your spirit is already speaking to you, too.
In the gut feelings you've overlooked.
In the dreams you can't shake.

In the coincidences that feel too perfect to shrug off. In the moments you "just happened" to be somewhere at the exact right time.

Your job isn't to force anything.
Your job is to listen — and honor the wisdom that rises.

The universe gives us signs. Have you been seeing a number repeatedly, does a topic keep coming up that means something to you, are you open to the signs the universe is trying to give you?

Your spiritual connection doesn't have to look like mine. It may not involve visions or dreams or synchronicities that feel like lightning. Yours might come through prayer, meditation, church, poetry, nature, music, journaling, tarot, movement, or quiet conversations with God at 3 a.m.

What matters isn't the method.
What matters is the openness.

So if you want to begin deepening your own spiritual life, can you start with any one of these things :

- Listen to your inner voice.
- Honor the nudge, even if it makes no sense yet.
- Create space — five minutes, ten minutes — to hear yourself.
- Say a prayer. Light a candle. Step outside and let the wind hit your skin.
- Ask for guidance and trust the first whisper that comes.

Spirit meets us where we are.
And when you take one step toward it, it takes ten toward you.

Traditional African spirituality teaches one core truth: Spirit is everywhere and always available. Whether you call it God, ancestors, intuition, energy, or something else, the connection is already within you. When you slow down, listen, and create space for that connection, you are practicing a form of spirituality that has guided our people for generations.

PART V

HEALING
FORWARD

One day you look up and realize—you survived.
That everything, even the parts that broke you open,
carried a purpose.
The bumps and bruises, the scrapes and cuts... none
of them stopped you.
You survived every relationship that ended, every job
that turned you away,
every moment that tried to convince you to shrink.

You kept digging deeper.
You kept moving forward.
You kept choosing yourself, even on the days it felt
impossible.

And you survived
because some part of you always knew
that one day...

you would turn your healing into freedom,
your story into power,
and your existence—
especially as a Black person in America—
into an act of resistance that could never be erased.

-Natasha Ickes

"What we heal in ourselves, we heal in the world."

— Marianne Williamson

Chapter 8

The Butterfly Effect

Healing is a lifelong journey. It doesn't end with a breakthrough, a journal entry, or a single moment of clarity. Healing is motion — forward, inward, upward. It's the steady reclaiming of everything life, trauma, and systems tried to take from you.

By the time you reach this chapter, you've traveled through history, memory, body, mind, and spirit. You've explored wounds you inherited and strengths you inherited too. You've learned the science behind belief, the power of breath, the wisdom of intuition, and the medicine carried in our communities, our ancestors, and our bodies.

But now comes the part no book can do for you:

Deciding what you will do with your healing. How will you heal forward?

Healing forward means choosing possibility where pain used to live.
It means imagining a life that isn't shaped by fear, survival, or shrinking — but by joy, alignment, rest, and intention.

It means understanding that healing is not the end of your story.
It is the beginning of your authorship.

A Vision for a Liberated Life

A liberated life doesn't mean a life without struggle.
It means a life where struggle no longer defines you.

It's:

- Choosing boundaries over burnout
- Choosing truth over silence
- Choosing community over isolation
- Choosing your own voice over the one the world tried to hand you
- Choosing ease where your ancestors only had endurance

Liberation is not a destination; it's a practice. A daily choosing of who you want to be, how you want to feel, and what legacy you want to leave behind.

And now you have tools to support that practice — tools rooted in culture, backed by science, shaped by your own lived experience.

A Network for Our Healing

I remember being a teenager, sitting in a dark movie theatre on opening night of *The Butterfly Effect*. Ashton Kutcher played a man haunted by his past, convinced that if he could just go back in time and fix one moment, everything would finally make sense. He believed that one choice — one different decision — would unravel all the pain that followed.

But every time he returned to the past and "fixed" one thing, something else unraveled.

He saved someone he loved... and someone else got hurt.

He prevented a tragedy... and created a different kind of heartbreak.

It was like watching someone rearrange pieces of a puzzle, only to realize the picture kept changing with every move. What he couldn't see — what most of us don't see when we're in survival mode — is that everything is connected. You can't tug on one thread without vibrating the whole web.

That movie stayed with me because it revealed something we don't always want to admit:

We are a part of a much larger system than we often recognize.

Our choices ripple further than we ever realize.

Our healing — or our avoidance of it — never affects only us.

Years later, I learned where the term *Butterfly Effect* actually came from.

It wasn't Hollywood — it was a meteorologist named Edward Lorenz in the 1960s.

One day, Lorenz ran a weather forecast model twice, but the second time he rounded one tiny decimal — something like .506127 instead of .506. A difference so small he assumed nothing would change. But the outcomes were completely different. The weather patterns shifted dramatically. He discovered that a tiny change in initial conditions can create massive, unpredictable effects later — like a butterfly flapping its wings in Brazil contributing to a tornado across the world. Not because the butterfly *caused* the tornado, but because small acts create chains of influence we can't see, measure, or predict. That idea shaped the entire field of chaos theory[66]. And honestly? It also shaped how I view healing.

Years later, in Laura Lynne Jackson's *Guided*, I learned about another scientist: Cleve Backster. He wasn't studying weather — he specialized in lie detection. One morning he hooked up his Dracaena plant to a polygraph, partly as a joke, partly out of curiosity. He wanted to see how long it would take for water to reach the leaves. At first, nothing happened.

Then Backster had a spontaneous thought: *What if I burn the leaf?*

He didn't touch the plant, didn't move toward it, didn't heat anything up — he simply *thought* about it.

The polygraph spiked so dramatically that Backster was shocked. It was as if the plant reacted to his intention — not his action. Could it be possible that this plant somehow knew or sensed what he planned to do?

Backster tested that theory with different scenarios. The most famous one being when he went into another room entirely, dropping live shrimp into boiling water. At the exact moment the shrimp were harmed, the machine attached to the plant registered a similar reaction[67].

Now, people have debated his research for years, but whether the plant felt pain, stress, or simply some kind of energetic shift, the message is the same:

Life responds to life.
Everything is connected — seen and unseen.
Everything we do ripples outward.

Our moods shift rooms.
Our words shift hearts.

Our presence shifts spaces.
Our intentions shift outcomes.

Some people walk into a room and the air tightens.
Others walk in and everyone exhales.

And we've all had that moment when someone's laugh, or hug, or simple eye contact didn't just change our day — it changed our spirit. This interconnectedness is not poetic. It's reality. It's physics, energy and a reminder that we are never alone.

So as I've explored how interconnected we truly are, I've found myself wanting to impact the world on multiple levels — through small moments and larger movements.

During the Trump administration, when racism grew louder and bolder, I felt suffocated by the hate. I found myself doubling down on love: giving more free haircuts in shelters, hugging my salon clients tighter, checking on my friends more often, holding my babies closer. All of that made me feel better. But still I felt the need to build a healing space for black people. One day it hit me: **The Black Healing Network.**

It began simply:

What if there was one central space where Black people could find Black therapists?

People who looked like them, understood their lived experience, and didn't need cultural footnotes to understand their pain?

But as I continued my graduate work, my clinical training, my community advocacy, and my own healing, I realized something:

It had to be *bigger*.

It had to honor the fullness of who we are — psychological, spiritual, communal, ancestral, embodied.
Not just therapy...
Not just resources...
Not just inspiration...

A home.
A hub.
A community of healing and liberation.

The Black Healing Network is a community-rooted movement dedicated to mental, emotional, and spiritual liberation for Black people. Built at the intersection of psychology, culture, and ancestral wisdom, its purpose is to:

- Increase access to culturally grounded mental health care by spotlighting Black therapists and healers.
- Provide education and tools for navigating trauma, racial stress, and emotional wellness.
- Create spaces — virtual and in-person — for connection, storytelling, and collective healing.
- Bridge modern psychology with ancient practices, honoring the traditions we've carried for generations.
- Empower individuals to heal themselves, their families, and their communities.

It's not a corporation, a clinic or a program. It's a movement — one that will grow as I grow, and evolve as we evolve.

As I step into my work as a therapist, my mission is simple:

To offer culturally grounded, trauma-informed care that sees the whole person — not just the symptoms.

Our ancestors healed in kitchens, in barbershops, in sanctuaries, in dance circles, in whispered prayers and loud laughter. We heal through community, through story, through presence.

This book is one doorway.
The Black Healing Network is another.

And my hope is that as you heal yourself, you'll ripple outward — touching lives you may never meet, shifting rooms you never enter, changing futures you'll never see.

That is the butterfly effect.
That is healing forward.
That is the legacy we're building together.

Your Turn: The Invitation

Healing forward isn't just about feeling better — it's about living differently. It's about asking yourself what becomes possible when survival is no longer your only goal. What do you build when you're no longer just trying to make it through the day, but imagining a life of meaning, joy, and expansion?

Legacy doesn't begin when we die. It begins in the choices we make while we're alive — the boundaries we set, the dreams we allow ourselves to want, the ways we model wholeness for those watching us. When you heal, you give the people who come after you permission to dream bigger, reach higher, and live more freely than you were ever taught to believe was possible.

You are not the person who opened this book. You've learned something. Released something. Questioned something. Remembered something.

Now, ask yourself:

- **What do I want to build from here?**
- **What part of my life is asking to be healed next?**
- **Who do I become when I am no longer surviving, but living?**

Healing forward means choosing yourself without apology.

It means honoring the whispers of your body, the wisdom of your mind, and the truth of your spirit.

It means understanding that you carry within you the resilience of those who came before you — and the freedom of those who will come after.

You are the bridge.

A Closing Blessing

May you trust your intuition like an old friend.
May your mind become a home instead of a
battlefield.

May you remember that healing is not something
you finish,
but something you practice — gently, daily,
imperfectly.

May your choices reflect who you are becoming,
not who you had to be to survive.

May your dreams stretch beyond what you were
taught to expect,
and may you give yourself permission to want more
—
more ease, more joy, more freedom, more life.

May you walk knowing that every step you take
toward wholeness
widens the path for those who come after you.

And may you never forget:

You are your ancestor's victory.
You are your own medicine.
You are the beginning of a new story.
Let's keep healing — forward.

"Your heart knows the way. Run in that direction."

- Rumi

References

1. CBS News. (1999, December 8). *MLK's family feels vindicated*. CBS News. https://www.cbsnews.com/news/mlks-family-feels-vindicated/

2. National Women's History Museum. (n.d.). *Rosa Parks*. https://www.womenshistory.org/education-resources/biographies/rosa-parks

3. Woods, M. (2017, October 13). *Mansa Musa, one of the wealthiest people who ever lived*. BBC. https://www.bbc.com/news/world-africa-37379425

4. Fiveable Inc. (n.d.). *African social and political structures*. In *Africa before 1800* (Unit 14 study guide). Retrieved from https://library.fiveable.me/africa-before-1800/unit-14

5. *Mamma Haidara Commemorative Library*. (n.d.). In *Wikipedia*. Retrieved [insert date], from https://en.wikipedia.org/wiki/Mamma_Haidara_Commemorative_Library

6. Hunwick, J. O. (1999). *Timbuktu and the Songhay Empire: Al-Sa'dN̄'s Ta ʾrN̄kh al-S¹dŌn down to 1613 and other contemporary documents.* Brill.

7. Egerton, D. R. (1993). *Gabriel's rebellion: The Virginia slave conspiracies of 1800 & 1802.* University of North Carolina Press.

8. Thornton, J. K. (1991). "African dimensions of the Stono Rebellion." *The American Historical Review, 96*(4), 1101–1113. https://doi.org/10.2307/2164990

9. Anderson, J. D. (2016). *Education and the Black struggle for equality.* In J. J. Hale (Ed.), *The state of Black America* (pp. 67–88). Transaction Publishers.

10. Rothstein, R. (2017). *The color of law: A forgotten history of how our government segregated America.* Liveright Publishing.

11. Wiltse, J. (2014). *Contested waters: A social history of swimming pools in America.* University of North Carolina Press

12. Daniel, P. (2013). *Dispossession: Discrimination against African American farmers in the age of civil rights.* University of North Carolina Press.

13. Reverby, S. M. (2009). *Examining Tuskegee: The infamous syphilis study and its legacy.* University of North Carolina Press.

14. Skloot, R. (2010). *The immortal life of Henrietta Lacks*. Crown Publishing Group.

15. Kuzawa, C. W., & Sweet, E. (2009). Epigenetics and the embodiment of race: Developmental origins of U.S. racial disparities in cardiovascular health. *American Journal of Human Biology, 21*(1), 2–15. https://doi.org/10.1002/ajhb.20822

16. Bilby, K. (2005). *True-Born Maroons*. University Press of Florida.

17. National Park Service. (2017, November 17). *Sojourner Truth: "Ain't I a Woman?"*. U.S. Department of the Interior.

18. Duster, M. A. (1994). *Ida: A Sword Among Lions*. Amistad. [Note: for Bessie Coleman, also see Rich, D. (1993). *Queen Bess: Daredevil Aviator*. National Women's History Museum.]

19. **Smith, W. A., Hung, M., & Franklin, J. D. (2011).** Racial battle fatigue and the misrecognition of African Americans in higher education and health contexts. *Equity & Excellence in Education, 44*(1), 31–48. https://doi.org/ 10.1080/10665684.2011.539472

20. Centers for Disease Control and Prevention. (2019, September 6). *Racial and ethnic disparities continue in pregnancy-related deaths.* U.S. Department of Health & Human Services. https://www.cdc.gov/media/releases/2019/p0905-racial-ethnic-disparities-pregnancy-deaths.html

21. Haskell, R. (2018, January 10). *Serena Williams on motherhood, marriage, and making her comeback.* Vogue. https://www.vogue.com/article/serena-williams-vogue-cover-interview-february-2018

22. Perry, A. M., Rothwell, J., & Harshbarger, D. (2018). **The devaluation of assets in Black neighborhoods: The case of residential property.** *Brookings Metropolitan Policy Program.*

23. McCargo, A., & Choi, J. H. (2020). https://www.urban.org/research/publication/closing-gaps-building-black-wealth-through-homeownership

24. Bertrand, M., & Mullainathan, S. (2004). Are Emily and Greg more employable than Lakisha and Jamal? A field experiment on labor market discrimination. *American*

25. U.S. Census Bureau. (2019, February 21). *Number of people with master's and doctoral degrees doubles since 2000.* America Counts. https://www.census.gov/content/dam/Census/newsroom/blogs/2019/degree-attainment.png

26. Forbes Business Council. (2024, July 5). *Why Black women are carving new career pathways as entrepreneurs. Forbes.*

27. Chen, Z., Pan, X., Bemben, M. G., & Bemben, D. A. (2011). Stronger bone correlates with African admixture in African-American women. *Journal of Bone and Mineral Research, 26*(2), 390–397. https://www.brookings.edu/research/ devaluation-of-assets-in-black-neighborhoods

28. Kapil, V., Weitzberg, E., Lundberg, J. O., & Ahluwalia, A. (2014). Clinical evidence demonstrating the utility of inorganic nitrate in cardiovascular health. *Nitric Oxide, 38,* 45–57. https://doi.org/10.1016/j.niox.2014.03.162

29. Smith, W. A., Hung, M., & Franklin, J. D. (2011). Racial battle fatigue and the miseducation of Black men: Racial microaggressions, societal problems, and environmental stress. *The Journal of Negro Education, 80*(1), 63–82.

30. Stanford Institute for Human-Centered Artificial Intelligence. (2022, March 9). *How social media shapes our perceptions about crime.* Stanford HAI.

31. Duxbury, S. W., Frizzell, L. C., & Lindsay, B. R. (2018). Mental illness, the media, and the moral politics of mass violence: The role of race in mass shootings coverage. *Journal of Research in Crime and Delinquency, 55*(6), 766–797. https://doi.org/10.1177/0022427818787225

32. California becomes first state to ban discrimination against natural hair. (2019, July 4). *Axios*.

33. Johns Hopkins Medicine. (2020, June 11). Keep your brain young with music. Johns Hopkins Medicine. https://www.hopkinsmedicine.org/health/wellness-and-prevention/keep-your-brain-young-with-music

34. Chanda, M. L., & Levitin, D. J. (2013). The neurochemistry of music. *Trends in Cognitive Sciences, 17*(4), 179–193. https://doi.org/10.1016/j.tics.2013.02.007

35. Hole, J., Hirsch, M., Ball, E., & Meads, C. (2015). Music as an aid for postoperative recovery in adults: A systematic review and meta-analysis. *The Lancet, 386*(10004), 1659–1671. https://doi.org/10.1016/S0140-6736(15)60169-6

36. Indiana University Lilly Family School of Philanthropy. (2012). Black households are more likely to give to charity than other groups, study finds. Indiana University. https://philanthropy.iupui.edu/news/national-study-of-philanthropy.html

37. Indiana University Lilly Family School of Philanthropy. (2025, June 4). *First-of-its-kind analysis of charitable giving to U.S. organizations serving communities of color reveals 2.9% of philanthropy supports these causes.* Retrieved from Indiana University website

38. Federal Bureau of Investigation. (1976). COINTELPRO: The FBI's covert action programs against American citizens. U.S. Senate Select Committee to Study Governmental Operations with Respect to Intelligence Activities (Church Committee), Final Report, Book III. https://www.intelligence.senate.gov/resources/intelligence-related-commissions

39. Ellsworth, S. (2001). *Death in a Promised Land: The Tulsa Race Riot of 1921.* Baton Rouge: Louisiana State University Press.

40. Ellsworth, S. (2001). *Death in a Promised Land: The Tulsa Race Riot of 1921.* Baton Rouge: Louisiana State University Press.

41. U.S. Census Bureau. (2021). *2020 Annual Business Survey: Employer firms by demographics.* Retrieved from https://www.census.gov

42. U.S. Census Bureau. (2021). *2020 Annual Business Survey: Employer firms by demographics.* Retrieved from https://www.census.gov

43. Gregory, A. (2022). Policing Jim Crow America: Enforcers' Agency and Structural Transformations. *Law & History Review*, 40(3), 501–533.

44. Tompson, T. (2013, August 1). *Public Mood in the U.S.: Significant Differences in Optimism Broken Down by Race.* AP-NORC Center for Public Affairs Research.

45. Moseley, J. B., O'Malley, K., Petersen, N. J., Menke, T. J., Brody, B. A., Kuykendall, D. H., Hollingsworth, J. C., Ashton, C. M., & Wray, N. P. (2002). A controlled trial of arthroscopic surgery for osteoarthritis of the knee. *New England Journal of Medicine, 347*(2), 81–88. https://doi.org/10.1056/NEJMoa013259

46. Klopfer, B. (1957). *Psychological variables in human cancer.* Journal of Projective Techniques, 21(3), 331–340.

47. de la Fuente-Fernández, R., Ruth, T. J., Sossi, V., Schulzer, M., Calne, D. B., & Stoessl, A. J. (2001). Expectation and dopamine release: Mechanism of the placebo effect in Parkinson's disease. *Science, 293*(5532), 1164–1166. https://doi.org/10.1126/science.1060937

48. Polusny, M. A., et al. (2015). Mindfulness-based stress reduction for PTSD among veterans. JAMA, 314(5), 456–465.

49. Ochsner, K. N., Bunge, S. A., Gross, J. J., & Gabrieli, J. D. (2002). Rethinking feelings: An fMRI study of the cognitive regulation of emotion. *Journal of Cognitive Neuroscience*, 14(8), 1215–1229.

50. Dickerson, S. S., & Kemeny, M. E. (2004). Acute stressors and cortisol responses: A theoretical integration and synthesis of laboratory research. Psychological Bulletin, 130(3), 355–391.https://doi.org/10.1037/0033-2909.130.3.355

51. Substance Abuse and Mental Health Services Administration. (2022). 2021 National Survey on Drug Use and Health: Racial/Ethnic Differences in Mental Health Service Use and Need for Services.https://www.samhsa.gov.

52. Copeland, W. E., Keeler, G., Angold, A., & Costello, E. J. (2007). *Traumatic events and posttraumatic stress in childhood.* Archives of General Psychiatry, 64(5), 577–584.

53. Yehuda, R., & Lehrner, A. (2018). Intergenerational transmission of trauma effects: Putative role of epigenetic mechanisms. *World Psychiatry, 17*(3), 243–257. https://doi.org/10.1002/wps.20568

54. McEwen B. S. (2017). Neurobiological and Systemic Effects of Chronic Stress. *Chronic stress (Thousand Oaks, Calif.), 1,* 2470547017692328. https://doi.org/10.1177/2470547017692328

55. American Psychological Association. (2018, November 1). *Stress effects on the body.* https://www.apa.org/topics/stress/body

56. Stojanovich, L., & Marisavljevich, D. (2008). *Stress as a trigger of autoimmune disease.* Autoimmunity Reviews, 7(3), 209–213. doi:10.1016/j.autrev.2007.11.007

57. Thayer, J. F., Åhs, F., Fredrikson, M., Sollers, J. J., & Wager, T. D. (2012). *A meta-analysis of heart rate variability and neuroimaging studies: Implications for vagal tone and stress regulation.* **Neuroscience &**

Biobehavioral Reviews, 36(2), 747–756. https://doi.org/10.1016/j.neubiorev.2011.11.009

58. Garcia-Gil, D., et al. (2020). *Effects of Tibetan singing bowl sound meditation on mood, anxiety, pain, and spiritual well-being: A randomized controlled trial.* Journal of Evidence-Based Integrative Medicine.

59. Buijze, G. A., Sierevelt, I. N., van Hellemondt, G. G., & van Dijk, C. N. (2019). *The effect of cold therapy on inflammation and recovery after exercise: A systematic review.* **American Journal of Sports Medicine, 47**(12), 2917–2926. https://doi.org/10.1177/0363546518808029

60. Chevalier, G., Sinatra, S. T., Oschman, J. L., Delany, R. M., & Sokal, K. (2012). *Earthing: Health implications of reconnecting the human body to the Earth's surface electrons.***Journal of Environmental and Public Health**, 2012, Article 291541. https://doi.org/10.1155/2012/291541

61. Food and Drug Administration. (2022). *Grade "A" pasteurized milk ordinance.* U.S. Department of Health and Human Services. https://www.fda. gov/food/dairy-guidance-documents-regulatory-information/grade-pasteurized-milk-ordinance

62. Humane Society of the United States. (2019). *An HSUS report: The reality behind "free-range" and "cage-free" labeling.* Washington, DC: HSUS.

63. Watson, N. F., Badr, M. S., Belenky, G., Bliwise, D. L., Buxton, O. M., Buysse, D., ... & Tasali, E. (2015). *Recommended amount of sleep for a healthy adult: A joint consensus statement of the American Academy of Sleep Medicine and Sleep Research Society.* Sleep, 38(6), 843–844.

64. Shokri-Kojori, E., Wang, G.-J., Wiers, C. E., Demiral, Ş. B., Guo, M., Kim, S. W., ... & Volkow, N. D. (2018). *β-Amyloid accumulation following sleep deprivation.* Proceedings of the National Academy of Sciences, 115(17), 4483–4488.

65. Oschman, J. L. (2015). *Energy medicine: The scientific basis* (2nd ed.). Edinburgh, UK: Churchill Livingstone.

66. Lorenz, E. N. (1963). Deterministic nonperiodic flow. *Journal of the Atmospheric Sciences, 20*(2), 130–141.

67. Backster, C. (2003). *Primary perception: Biocommunication with plants, living foods, and human cells.* White Rose Millennium Press. Oschman, J. L. (2015). *Energy medicine: The scientific basis* (2nd ed.). Edinburgh, UK: Churchill Livingstone.

www.ingramcontent.com/pod-product-compliance
Lightning Source LLC
Chambersburg PA
CBHW062057080426
42734CB00012B/2675